RUTH
TALK

RUTH

Questions & Answers
on the Book of Ruth

TALK

Moshe Pinchas Weisblum

 JONATHAN DAVID PUBLISHERS, INC.
Middle Village, New York 11379

Jonathan David Publishers, Inc.
68-22 Eliot Avenue
Middle Village, New York 11379

www.jdbooks.com

2 4 6 8 10 9 7 5 3 1

Library of Congress Cataloging-in-Publication Data

Weisblum, Moshe Pinchas.
  Ruth talk : questions and answers on the book of Ruth / by Moshe
Pinchas Weisblum.
      p. cm.
  ISBN 0-8246-0461-X
  1. Bible. O.T. Ruth—Criticism, interpretation, etc. I. Title.

BS1315.52.V57 2005
222'.3506—dc22
                                                          2004059379

Book design and composition by John Reinhardt Book Design

Printed in the United States of America

This book is dedicated to our son, Eric S. Kinzbrunner, in honor of his graduation from the United States Naval Academy in Annapolis, Maryland, and his commissioning as an ensign in the United States Navy in May 2004.

This book also is dedicated with gratitude to the author, Rabbi Moshe Pinchas Weisblum, whose kindness and support were instrumental in ensuring that Eric could continue to properly observe Torah and mitzvot during his four years as a midshipman at the Naval Academy.

Rabbi Dr. Barry and Anita Kinzbrunner

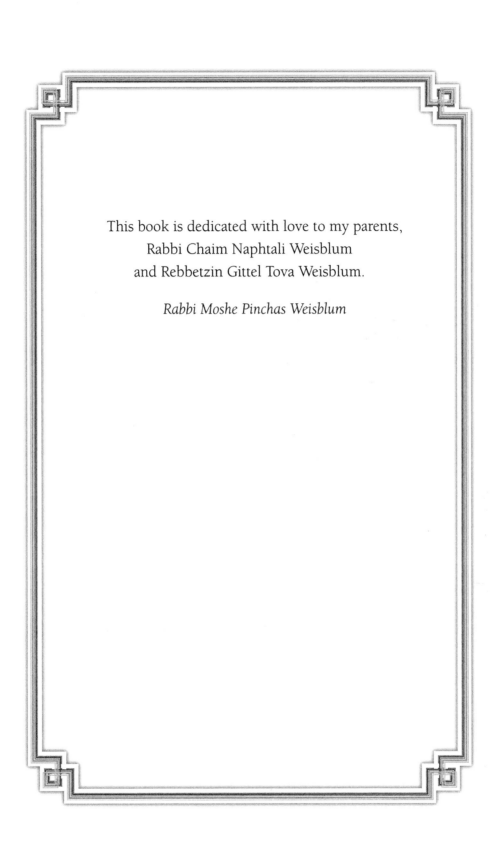

This book is dedicated with love to my parents,
Rabbi Chaim Naphtali Weisblum
and Rebbetzin Gittel Tova Weisblum.

Rabbi Moshe Pinchas Weisblum

Contents

Acknowledgments

Thank You, Almighty God, for the kindness You have bestowed upon me and my family.

I acknowledge with gratitude all those who assisted me with this book, and without whom this project would not have come to fruition:

To my father, Rabbi Chaim Naphtali Weisblum, of Neva Shanan, Haifa, Israel, and my mother, Rebbetzin Gittel Tova Weisblum, for their encouragement and love.

To my mother-in-law, Rebbetzin Devorah HaEitan, for her strength and love.

To my wife, Miriam, and to our children, Elimelech, Bracha, Ayala Chana, Yitzhak Meir, and Natan, whose devotion and constant support made it possible for me to undertake *Ruth Talk*.

To my extended family and to my teachers, for their wisdom and guidance.

To Judith Sandman, whose editing skills enhanced the quality of this work.

To my entire congregation, Kneseth Israel, in Annapolis, Maryland, President Singerman, and Rebbetzin Esther Rosenblatt for their friendship and advice.

To Susan Roth my deepest thanks for her encouragement and support.

To Dr. Shimon Shokek for his wisdom and instruction.

To Arthur Kurzweil for his suggestions and guidance.

Thanks, too, to Rebbetzin Adele Bernstein, Dr. Bruce Friedman, Rabbi Ezra Admoni, Rabbi Barry Freundel, Rabbi Nesanel Kostelitz, Dr. Aharon Weisberg, Henya Storch, Yael Resnick, Dr. Leonard and Mrs. Ruth Ginsberg, Cantor Moshe Bazian, Jacob Lebow, and Kenneth Hartwell for their kind assistance and insightful comments.

A special expression of gratitude to David Kolatch, Marvin Sekler, and Rachel Taller of Jonathan David Publishers, whose professionalism made working on this project a pleasure.

To all of my students for the opportunity to study together and exchange ideas.

And to you, my readers, for joining me on this journey. May God bless us all.

—Rabbi Moshe Pinchas Weisblum

Preface

We all share the desire to learn the secrets of the past. Through ancient tales of universal human experience, of struggle and hope, sorrow and victory, we can incorporate the lessons of the past into our own lives today.

The first book that I published in English, *Table Talk: Biblical Questions and Answers*, was crafted as a friendly road map to the Torah—the five books of Moses. Thankfully, the book was well received and has been reprinted several times. Encouraged by the positive feedback and driven by a deeply felt desire to transmit Jewish classics to a new generation of readers, I turned to the *Book of Ruth*.

They say that good things come in small packages, and while the three-thousand-year-old *Book of Ruth* is only four chapters long, it is a petite literary gem filled with lessons as valuable to us today as they were to ancient readers. My aim in *Ruth Talk* is to provide food for spiritual thought, mining each verse of the *Book of Ruth* to reveal the central themes and motifs of this beautiful work: kindness, humility, choice, fate, and, above all, *tikkun olam*—repairing the world. The hand of God guides our every move, but God has put the Torah into *our* hands to help us make the right decisions. Should we stray from the proper path, the *Book of Ruth* demonstrates that it is never too late to turn around, ask for directions, and get on the right road; and as Ruth herself demonstrates, the actions of a single human being can change the course of history.

Tikkun Olam

Transforming ourselves, helping those around us, and contributing to the betterment of the world are at the heart of the *Book of Ruth* and are all aspects of *tikkun olam*.

Tikkun olam literally means "repairing the world." Moses Maimonides, the great twelfth-century Jewish philosopher and physician known as the Rambam, believed that the more a person devotes him- or herself to study and to the performance of the mitzvot—the commandments—of the Torah, the greater one's contribution to repairing the flawed world in which we live.

The sixteenth-century kabbalist, Rabbi Yitzchak Luria of Safed, Israel, known as the Ari—the Lion—and one of the most influential figures in Jewish mysticism, explains *tikkun olam* much more elaborately. When God created the world, Rabbi Luria taught, the world could not contain all of His abundant light, so God contracted His radiance and stowed it in specially prepared holy vessels. God's light was so brilliant, however, that the vessels themselves shattered, splintering into millions of pieces like dishes dropped on the floor, scattering God's divine sparks. The purpose of existence, declared Rabbi

Luria, is to restore the world to the state of perfection in which it existed at the time of Creation. This can be accomplished through *tikkun olam*—finding what is broken in the world and repairing it.

The Mishnah teaches in *Pirkei Avot*—*Ethics of the Fathers*—that the world rests on three pillars: Torah, service to God, and *gemilut chasadim*—acts of loving-kindness (*Avot* 1:2). Ruth, the heroine of our story, who renounced the religion of her birth and embraced Judaism; who unhesitatingly devoted herself to the care of her widowed mother-in-law, though her own husband had just died; and whose deeds of loving-kindness merited that she would marry Boaz and become the great-grandmother of King David, who would build the First Temple and from whose line, it is said, the Messiah will one day descend, exemplified all of these qualities—devotion to Torah, service to God, and the performance of acts of *chesed*. The trip upon which Ruth embarked, accompanying her mother-in-law, Naomi, from the country of Moab to the city of Bethlehem, in Israel, represented far more than a physical journey. It was a spiritual journey, a journey of self-transformation.

Full Circle

The patriarch Abraham was the first Jew; the Midrash—the lessons of the Sages—teaches that Ruth was the first individual to convert to Judaism. Abraham was distinguished for his many acts of *chesed*, notable among them, hospitality; Ruth also embodied *chesed*, and this attribute motivated her every action. In tracing Ruth's distant origins back to Abraham's own, and forward to her decision to join the Jewish people, a circle is completed, and the reader can begin to understand how important the choices one makes in life are in determining the kind of person he or she will become.

The Torah tells us that when God commanded Abraham to leave the land of his birth and journey to Canaan—the Promised Land—he was accompanied not only by his wife Sarah, but by his nephew Lot, whom he had taken into his household when Haran, his brother and Lot's father, had died.

Lot traveled with Abraham and lived with him for many years, until a quarrel broke out between their shepherds. Lot and Abraham agreed to part company, and Abraham gave Lot first choice of territory. Lot picked the fertile Jordan plain, settling in the city of Sodom.

When Abraham was ninety-nine years old, God commanded him to circumcise himself and the other males in his household. Soon after, as Abraham was recovering from the circumcision, he was visited by three travelers. Although in pain, Abraham hastened to greet his guests, urging them to relax in the shade and preparing a feast for them to eat. Before they departed, they revealed to him that they were actually angels and were on their way to Sodom and Gomorrah to destroy those cities of evil.

Though Abraham bargained vigorously with God to spare the citizens of Sodom and Gomorrah, not even ten righteous individuals could be found among the cities' inhabitants, and God proceeded with his plans to blot them out, agreeing, however, to spare Lot and his wife and children.

A small vestige of Abraham's hospitality had obviously rubbed off on Lot, for when the angels arrived in Sodom, still disguised as weary travelers, Lot urged them to spend the night in his house. And when the townspeople pounded on Lot's door, demanding that he turn over his visitors to the seething mob, he refused. In order to pacify the townspeople, Lot volunteered to send out his virgin daughters, but the travelers pulled Lot back inside his house, where they warned him to gather up his family and flee because God's punishment would soon rain down on Sodom and Gomorrah.

Lot's wife disobeyed God's order not to look back at the burning cities and was turned into a pillar of salt. Lot and his two daughters hid in a cave. Believing that the entire world had been obliterated and they were the only survivors, the young women got Lot drunk and had intimate relations with him. Both daughters gave birth to sons, one named Moab, the other named Ben-ammi, who became the fathers of the Moabite and Ammonite nations.

The theme of hospitality—or a lack of it—arises again several generations later, following the Exodus from Egypt, when the Israelites, hungry and thirsty, camped on the plains of Moab. The Moabites refused to share even bread and water with the Jews, and because of this, Jews were eternally prohibited from marrying Moabites or Ammonites.

Fast-forwarding again, what country could be more

attractive to a family of hoarders than Moab, the land known for its selfish, avaricious inhabitants? This is precisely what Elimelech thought to himself when famine struck the land of Israel, and he and his wife, Naomi, and their sons fled Bethlehem to Moab to elude their needy Jewish neighbors.

Elimelech soon died in Moab, and his sons, Mahlon and Chilion, married Moabite women, Ruth and Orpah, but not just any women, daughters of Eglon, the king of Moab. Ten years later Mahlon and Chilion died, leaving their wives and mother destitute.

When Naomi learned that the famine had ended in Israel, she decided to return home to Bethlehem but urged her daughters-in-law to remain in Moab, the land of their birth. Orpah, after much persuasion, agreed to stay. But what about Ruth?

Let us imagine Ruth immediately after the death of her husband. According to the Midrash, Naomi, Ruth, and Orpah, previously high-ranking, wealthy women, were left penniless when Mahlon and Chilion died— the women could not even afford shrouds in which to bury their dead. Naomi had no other children to console her; Orpah and Ruth were childless, as well. Had our text described Ruth throwing herself on the ground and beating her breast in grief, or secluding herself in her home, or even returning to her parents' home, we would have understood: any of these would have been natural responses to the terrible tragedy that had befallen her—and exactly what we would have expected of a Moabite.

Breaking with everything she knew, Ruth set a fresh course for herself, one that would ultimately carry her back to her Jewish roots.

We Will Act and We Will Hear

We read *Megillat Rut,* the *Book of Ruth,* on Shavuot, a holiday known by many names. God commands us in *Leviticus* 23:15 to count seven weeks—forty-nine days—from the second day of Passover, and on the fiftieth day to observe the Festival of Weeks (Shavuot in Hebrew means "weeks"). Shavuot also is called Yom ha-Bikkurim, Day of the First Fruits, for it was on this day that the first fruits of the grain harvest were brought to the Temple in Jerusalem. Most importantly, Shavuot is Zeman Mattan Toratenu, the Time of the Giving of Our Torah, for it was on this day that God gave the Jews the Torah on Mount Sinai.

Our Sages teach that before God gave the Torah to the Jewish people, He offered it to the other nations of the world. That way, they wouldn't be able to say, "If only you had offered the Torah to us first, we gladly would have accepted it."

The first nation to whom God offered the Torah said, "Tell us what is in it." God answered, "You shall not murder." "We can't accept that," they replied. "We are a nation of warriors."

God approached another nation. "What's in this Torah of yours?" they asked. God answered, "You shall not steal." "Not steal?" the people scoffed. "How do you think we have amassed such great wealth? By stealing from others, of course!"

In this way, all seventy nations of the world rejected the Torah. Finally, God approached the Israelites. "What is in the Torah?" they asked. "Six hundred and thirteen commandments," said God. *Na'aseh ve-nishma.* "We will act, and we will hear!" replied the children of Israel firmly. So eager were they to receive God's Torah that they immediately accepted it, and only then did they ask for the details. Like the Jews who answered *Na'aseh ve-nishma*, Ruth, too, acted decisively when Mahlon, her husband, died.

One of the greatest acts of kindness a person can perform is burying the dead, for it is a deed that cannot be repaid. And that is exactly what Ruth did: Mahlon needed to be buried, so Ruth buried him. It was unheard of for a woman to travel alone, so Ruth accompanied Naomi to Bethlehem; along the way, Naomi taught Ruth, who was determined to convert to Judaism, everything she needed to know about the Jewish faith. Upon reaching the city, Naomi and Ruth needed to eat, so Ruth immediately set out to the fields to glean grain. Naomi instructed Ruth to go to Boaz at night on the threshing room floor, so Ruth did; when another relative rejected the opportunity to redeem Elimelech's property and marry Ruth, Ruth married Boaz and immediately conceived their son, Obed.

The Hebrew expression *mitzvah goreret mitzvah va-averah goreret averah*, "one good deed leads to another and one sin to a second," is borne out by the stories of Lot and Ruth. Each sin that Lot committed took him further away from the ideals his uncle had tried to instill in him; each act of *chesed* performed by Ruth led to another—and greater—act of *chesed.*

Our Sages teach that there are two kinds of *tikkun*—*tikkun perati,* "personal *tikkun,*" those mitzvot and acts of *chesed* that help us better ourselves; and *tikkun kelali,*" "communal *tikkun,*" those mitzvot and acts of *chesed* we perform that help those around us—both of which contribute to *tikkun olam,* repairing the whole world. Ruth's conversion and commitment to Judaism, and the numerous acts of *chesed* she performed embraced both *tikkun perati* and *tikkun kelali.* As we sing on Pesach, *Dayyenu,* "That would have been enough." But what makes Ruth even more exemplary—and a model for us today!—is that her actions inspired those around her to *tikkun olam,* in particular, Naomi and Boaz.

Political Posturing

The message of the *Book of Ruth* that resonates most clearly for readers today is *tikkun olam.* But it would be disingenuous to argue that this was the prophet Samuel's sole reason for writing the *Book of Ruth* three thousand years ago: in addition to the moral message Samuel wished to convey to the Israelites was an important political message that needed to be delivered.

Every Jewish child is taught to sing the Hebrew song "*David, Melech Yisra'el,*" whose words mean, "David, king of Israel, lives forever." Great-grandson of Ruth and Boaz, forebear of the Messiah, David is considered Israel's greatest statesman, warrior, and poet. Yet, three thousand years ago, his legacy was hardly assured; King

Saul, Israel's first monarch, egged on by his closest advisor, Doeg, questioned David's legitimacy to succeed him to the throne on the pretext that David's great-grandmother, Ruth, was a Moabite.

Between the death of Joshua, who succeeded Moses, and the institution of the monarchy, ancient Israel was served by a series of judges. During this period, the Israelites often strayed into idolatrous worship and battled incursions from neighboring countries—punishment from God for their religious lapses.

The first chapter of *1 Samuel* records the desperate prayer of Hannah, wife of Elkanah, for a child. If her prayer was granted, she vowed to consecrate her son to the sanctuary at Shiloh. Hannah was blessed with Samuel, and delivered him, as promised, to the care of Eli, the high priest and judge. Samuel would serve as the last of the judges and was responsible for the transformation of Israel from a loose confederacy of tribes into a monarchy.

Initially, Samuel rejected the pleas of the Israelites for a king, arguing that God was the only king of Israel. But increasingly bloody clashes with the Philistines led the Israelites to demand a king more vociferously. *1 Samuel* 8:22 records the words God spoke to Samuel: "Heed their demands and appoint a king for them." Samuel anointed Saul, who established Gibeah as his capital and strove to secure the borders of Israel against the Moabites, Ammonites, Edomites, and Philistines. The relationship between Samuel and Saul was always strained; Saul's failure to heed Samuel's instructions and utterly destroy the Amalekites, leaving no survivors, marked the final breach, and, unbeknownst to Saul, Samuel secretly anointed David to be the future king.

At first Saul was charmed by the young David, a skilled musician and a crafty warrior who defeated the Philistine giant Goliath with a simple slingshot. As David's renown spread, Saul grew increasingly jealous. *1 Samuel* 18:7 records the song sung by the women who greeted David upon his return from battle: "Saul has slain his thousands, David, his tens of thousands." Saul tried to kill David a number of times, but in a message from beyond the grave, Samuel foretold the death of Saul and his sons in the battle of Gilboa, after which David was crowned king.

Though the Torah expressly forbids Israelites from marrying Moabites, the *Book of Ruth* makes crystal clear that this prohibition applied only to Israelite women who wished to marry Moabite men. Israelite men who wished to marry Moabite women who had converted to Judaism, as had Ruth, were permitted to do so, and not just any Israelite men. Ruth married Boaz, a pillar of Bethlehem society, a man who scrupulously observed Jewish law, a judge, a landowner, a philanthropist. A pious woman in her own right, whose marriage to Boaz elevated them both, Ruth merited having King David for a great-grandson, and David, "...son of Jesse...skilled in music...a stalwart fellow and a warrior, sensible in speech, and handsome in appearance, and whom the Lord is with" (*1 Samuel* 16:18), merited having Ruth for his great-grandmother.

Written Law, Oral Law

The prohibition against Israelites marrying Moabites or Ammonites in *Deuteronomy* 23:4–5 reads as follows:

> No Ammonite or Moabite shall be admitted into the congregation of the Lord; none of their descendants, even in the tenth generation, shall ever be admitted into the congregation of the Lord, because they did not meet you with food and water on your journey after you left Egypt, and because they hired Balaam son of Beor... to curse you.

We said above that this prohibition applied only to Israelite women who wished to marry Moabite men, but not to Israelite men who wished to marry Moabite women. Since the Torah does not say this specifically, how do we know that this was so? Contained in the political tutorial that David was the legitimate successor to Saul lies a pivotal religious doctrine, as well.

What did the Jews receive at Mount Sinai? If you answered only the Ten Commandments, you would be wrong. The revelation at Mount Sinai, our tradition teaches, encompassed not just the giving of the Ten Commandments, nor even the giving of the written law (*Torah she-bi-khetav*), but the giving of the complete written *and* oral law (*Torah she-be-al peh*), which explicates the written law and without which it would be impossible to carry out the commandments of the *Torah she-bi-khetav*, since the details of their observance are not spelled out in the written text.

Although the classical texts of the oral law—the Mishnah, which was compiled in approximately 200 C.E., and the Talmud, in which are collected the teachings of the great rabbis who lived between 200 and 500 C.E.—obviously postdate the giving of the Torah on Mount Sinai, Jewish tradition teaches that the oral law has existed as long as the written law.

Shavuot

There are many lovely traditions associated with the festival of Shavuot, including eating dairy foods and decorating our homes and synagogues with greenery. It is said that until the Jewish nation received the Torah, the people did not know the Jewish dietary rules—the laws of kashrut; therefore, on the day on which they received the Torah from God, they refrained from eating meat and ate only dairy foods, as a way of preparing to undertake the new mitzvot they would receive. Similarly, Ruth went through a process of spiritual purification, putting Moab, literally and figuratively, behind her, and preparing to accept God's word, the Torah.

We decorate our homes and synagogues with greenery to remind us that the giving of the Torah took place on a mountain abloom with flowers and plants. Ruth was reborn and blossomed in the Jewish faith; in giving birth to Obed, who would father Jesse, who would father David, the cycle of life came full circle and continues to turn.

A third tradition associated with Shavuot is Torah study. Typically, we pull an all-nighter—immersing ourselves (on the first night in the Diaspora) in study and prayer from late night to early morning.

I sincerely hope that *Ruth Talk* will help you keep your eyes open, your mind moving, and your soul ignited, whether you study the *Book of Ruth* in the synagogue or at home, alone or in a group. The Sages teach that the more hours we study Torah on Shavuot, the more holiness that enters the world. May *Ruth Talk* deepen your understanding of *Megillat Rut*—the *Book of Ruth*—and enrich your celebration of Zeman Mattan Toratenu—the Time of the Giving of Our Torah.

The Book of Ruth
in English Translation

1 In the days when the chieftains[a] ruled, there was a famine in the land; and a man of Bethlehem in Judah, with his wife and two sons, went to reside in the country of Moab. ²The man's name was Elimelech, his wife's name was Naomi, and his two sons were named Mahlon and Chilion—Ephrathites of Bethlehem in Judah. They came to the country of Moab and remained there.

³Elimelech, Naomi's husband, died; and she was left with her two sons. ⁴They married Moabite women, one named Orpah and the other Ruth, and they lived there about ten years. ⁵Then those two—Mahlon and Chilion—also died; so the woman was left without her two sons and without her husband.

⁶She started out with her daughters-in-law to return from the country of Moab; for in the country of Moab she had heard that the LORD had taken note of His people and given them food. ⁷Accompanied by her two daugh-

Reprinted from *Tanakh*, © 1985, The Jewish Publication Society with the permission of the publisher, The Jewish Publication Society. All quotations from the *Book of Ruth* that appear in *Ruth Talk* follow the JPS translation. A complete translation is included here for readers' reference.

[a] *I.e., the leaders who arose in the period before the monarchy; others "judges."*

ters-in-law, she left the place where she had been living; and they set out on the road back to the land of Judah.

⁸But Naomi said to her two daughters-in-law, "Turn back, each of you to her mother's house. May the LORD deal kindly with you, as you have dealt with the dead and with me! ⁹May the LORD grant that each of you find security in the house of a husband!" And she kissed them farewell. They broke into weeping ¹⁰and said to her, "No, we will return with you to your people."

¹¹But Naomi replied, "Turn back, my daughters! Why should you go with me? Have I any more sons in my body who might be husbands for you? ¹²Turn back, my daughters, for I am too old to be married. Even if I thought there was hope for me, even if I were married tonight and I also bore sons, ¹³should you wait for them to grow up? Should you on their account debar your-selves from marriage? Oh no, my daughters! My lot is far more bitter than yours, for the hand of the LORD has struck out against me."

¹⁴They broke into weeping again, and Orpah kissed her mother-in-law farewell. But Ruth clung to her. ¹⁵So she said, "See, your sister-in-law has returned to her people and her gods. Go follow your sister-in-law." ¹⁶But Ruth replied, "Do not urge me to leave you, to turn back and not follow you. For wherever you go, I will go; wherever you lodge, I will lodge; your people shall be my people, and your God my God. ¹⁷Where you die, I will die, and there I will be buried. ᵇ⁻Thus and more may

---

ᵇ⁻ᵇ *A formula of imprecation.*

the Lord do to me[b] if anything but death parts me from you." 18When [Naomi] saw how determined she was to go with her, she ceased to argue with her; 19and the two went on until they reached Bethlehem.

When they arrived in Bethlehem, the whole city buzzed with excitement over them. The women said, "Can this be Naomi?" 20"Do not call me Naomi,"[c] she replied. "Call me Mara,[d] for Shaddai[e] has made my lot very bitter. 21I went away full, and the Lord has brought me back empty. How can you call me Naomi, when the Lord has [f-]dealt harshly with[-f] me, when Shaddai has brought misfortune upon me!"

22Thus Naomi returned from the country of Moab; she returned with her daughter-in-law Ruth the Moabite. They arrived in Bethlehem at the beginning of the barley harvest.

2 Now Naomi had a kinsman on her husband's side, a man of substance, of the family of Elimelech, whose name was Boaz.

2Ruth the Moabite said to Naomi, "I would like to go to the fields and glean among the ears of grain, behind someone who may show me kindness." "Yes, daughter, go," she replied; 3and off she went. She came and gleaned in a field, behind the reapers; and, as luck would have it, it was the piece of land belonging to Boaz, who was

---

[c] I.e., "Pleasantness."

[d] I.e., "Bitterness."

[e] Usually rendered "the Almighty."

[f-f] Others "testified against."

of Elimelech's family.

⁴Presently Boaz arrived from Bethlehem. He greeted the reapers, "The LORD be with you!" And they responded, "The LORD bless you!" ⁵Boaz said to the servant who was in charge of the reapers, "Whose girl is that?" ⁶The servant in charge of the reapers replied, "She is a Moabite girl who came back with Naomi from the country of Moab. ⁷She said, 'Please let me glean and gather among the sheaves behind the reapers.' She has been on her feet ever since she came this morning. *a*-She has rested but little in the hut."-*a*

⁸Boaz said to Ruth, *b*-"Listen to me, daughter.-*b* Don't go to glean in another field. Don't go elsewhere, but stay here close to my girls. ⁹Keep your eyes on the field they are reaping, and follow them. I have ordered the men not to molest you. And when you are thirsty, go to the jars and drink some of [the water] that the men have drawn."

¹⁰She prostrated herself with her face to the ground, and said to him, "Why are you so kind as to single me out, when I am a foreigner?"

¹¹Boaz said in reply, "I have been told of all that you did for your mother-in-law after the death of your husband, how you left your father and mother and the land of your birth and came to a people you had not known before. ¹²May the LORD reward your deeds. May you have a full recompense from the LORD, the God of Israel, under whose wings you have sought refuge!"

---

a-a Meaning of Heb. uncertain.
b-b Lit. "Have you not heard, daughter?"

¹³She answered, "You are most kind, my lord, to comfort me and to speak gently to your maidservant—though I am not so much as one of your maidservants."

¹⁴At mealtime, Boaz said to her, "Come over here and partake of the meal, and dip your morsel in the vinegar." So she sat down beside the reapers. He handed her roasted grain, and she ate her fill and had some left over.

¹⁵When she got up again to glean, Boaz gave orders to his workers, "You are not only to let her glean among the sheaves, without interference, ¹⁶but you must also pull some [stalks] out of the heaps and leave them for her to glean, and not scold her."

¹⁷She gleaned in the field until evening. Then she beat out what she had gleaned—it was about an *ephah* of barley—¹⁸and carried it back with her to the town. When her mother-in-law saw what she had gleaned, and when she also took out and gave her what she had left over after eating her fill, ¹⁹her mother-in-law asked her, "Where did you glean today? Where did you work? Blessed be he who took such generous notice of you!" So she told her mother-in-law whom she had worked with, saying, "The name of the man with whom I worked today is Boaz."

²⁰Naomi said to her daughter-in-law, "Blessed be he of the LORD, who has not failed in His kindness to the living or to the dead! For," Naomi explained to her daughter-in-law, "the man is related to us; he is one of our redeeming kinsmen."ᶜ ²¹Ruth the Moabite said, "He even told me, 'Stay close by my workers until all my harvest is

---

ᶜ Cf. Lev. 25.25 and note and Deut. 25.5–6. The fact that Boaz was a kinsman of Ruth's dead husband opened up the possibility of providing an heir for the latter.

finished.'" ²²And Naomi answered her daughter-in-law Ruth, "It is best, daughter, that you go out with his girls, and not be annoyed in some other field." ²³So she stayed close to the maidservants of Boaz, and gleaned until the barley harvest and the wheat harvest were finished. Then she stayed at home with her mother-in-law.

3 Naomi, her mother-in-law, said to her, "Daughter, I must seek a home for you, where you may be happy. ²Now there is our kinsman Boaz, whose girls you were close to. He will be winnowing barley on the threshing floor tonight. ³So bathe, anoint yourself, dress up, and go down to the threshing floor. But do not disclose yourself to the man until he has finished eating and drinking. ⁴When he lies down, note the place where he lies down, and go over and uncover his feet and lie down. He will tell you what you are to do." ⁵She replied, "I will do everything you tell me."

⁶She went down to the threshing floor and did just as her mother-in-law had instructed her. ⁷Boaz ate and drank, and in a cheerful mood went to lie down beside the grainpile. Then she went over stealthily and uncovered his feet and lay down. ⁸In the middle of the night, the man gave a start and pulled back—there was a woman lying at his feet!

⁹"Who are you?" he asked. And she replied, "I am your handmaid Ruth. ^{a-}Spread your robe over your handmaid,^{-a} for you are a redeeming kinsman."

_____

^{a-a} *A formal act of espousal; cf. Ezek. 16.8.*

¹⁰He exclaimed, "Be blessed of the LORD, daughter! Your latest deed of loyalty is greater than the first, in that you have not turned to younger men, whether poor or rich.ᵇ ¹¹And now, daughter, have no fear. I will do in your behalf whatever you ask, for all the ᶜelders of my townᶜ know what a fine woman you are. ¹²But while it is true I am a redeeming kinsman, there is another redeemer closer than I. ¹³Stay for the night. Then in the morning, if he will act as a redeemer, good! let him redeem. But if he does not want to act as redeemer for you, I will do so myself, as the LORD lives! Lie down until morning."

¹⁴So she lay at his feet until dawn. She rose before one person could distinguish another, for he thought, "Let it not be known that the woman came to the threshing floor." ¹⁵And he said, "Hold out the shawl you are wearing." She held it while he measured out six measures of barley, and he put it on her back.

When sheᵈ got back to the town, ¹⁶she came to her mother-in-law, who asked, "How is it with you, daughter?" She told her all that the man had done for her; ¹⁷and she added, "He gave me these six measures of barley, saying to me, 'Do not go back to your mother-in-law empty-handed.'" ¹⁸And Naomi said, "Stay here, daughter, till you learn how the matter turns out. For the man will not rest, but will settle the matter today."

ᵇ I.e., she sought out a kinsman of her dead husband; see note at 2.20 above. Her first act of loyalty had been to return with Naomi.

ᶜ⁻ᶜ Lit. "gate of my people."

ᵈ So in many Heb. mss; most mss. read "he."

4 Meanwhile, Boaz had gone to the gate and sat down there. And now the redeemer whom Boaz had mentioned passed by. He called, "Come over and sit down here, so-and-so!" And he came over and sat down. ²Then [Boaz] took ten elders of the town and said, "Be seated here"; and they sat down.

³He said to the redeemer, "Naomi, now returned from the country of Moab, must sell the piece of land which belonged to our kinsman Elimelech. ⁴I thought I should disclose the matter to you and say: Acquire it in the presence of those seated here and in the presence of the elders of my people. If you are willing to redeem it, redeem! But if you*ᵃ* will not redeem, tell me, that I may know. For there is no one to redeem but you, and I come after you." "I am willing to redeem it," he replied. ⁵Boaz continued, "When you acquire the property from Naomi *ᵇ⁻*and from Ruth the Moabite, you must also acquire the wife of the deceased,*⁻ᵇ* so as to perpetuate the name of the deceased upon his estate." ⁶The redeemer replied, "Then I cannot redeem it for myself, lest I impair my own estate.*ᶜ* You take over my right of redemption, for I am unable to exercise it."

⁷Now this was formerly done in Israel in cases of redemption or exchange: to validate any transaction, one man would take off his sandal and hand it to the other.

ᵃ So many Heb. mss., Septuagint, and Targum; most mss. read "he."

ᵇ⁻ᵇ Emendation yields "you must also acquire Ruth the Moabite, the wife of the deceased"; cf. v. 10.

ᶜ I.e., by expending capital for property which will go to the son legally regarded as Mahlon's; see Deut. 25.5–6.

Such was the practice[d] in Israel. [8]So when the redeemer said to Boaz, "Acquire for yourself," he drew off his sandal. [9]And Boaz said to the elders and to the rest of the people, "You are witnesses today that I am acquiring from Naomi all that belonged to Elimelech and all that belonged to Chilion and Mahlon. [10]I am also acquiring Ruth the Moabite, the wife of Mahlon, as my wife, so as to perpetuate the name of the deceased upon his estate, that the name of the deceased may not disappear from among his kinsmen and from the gate of his home town. You are witnesses today."

[11]All the people at the gate and the elders answered, "We are. May the LORD make the woman who is coming into your house like Rachel and Leah, both of whom built up the House of Israel! Prosper in Ephrathah[e] and perpetuate your name in Bethlehem! [12]And may your house be like the house of Perez whom Tamar bore to Judah—through the offspring which the LORD will give you by this young woman."

[13]So Boaz married Ruth; she became his wife, and he cohabited with her. The LORD let her conceive, and she bore a son. [14]And the women said to Naomi, "Blessed be the LORD, who has not withheld a redeemer from you today! May his name be perpetuated in Israel! [15]He will renew your life and sustain your old age; for he is born of your daughter-in-law, who loves you and is better to you than seven sons."

---

[d] *Understanding Heb. te'udah in the sense of the Arabic 'âdah and Syriac 'yâdâ. Cf. Ibn Ezra.*

[e] *Ephrathah is another name applied to Bethlehem; cf. 1.2; Gen. 35.16, 19; 48.7; Mic. 5.1.*

¹⁶Naomi took the child and held it to her bosom. She became its foster mother, ¹⁷and the women neighbors gave him a name, saying, "A son is born to Naomi!" They named him Obed; he was the father of Jesse, father of David.

¹⁸This is the line of Perez: Perez begot Hezron, ¹⁹Hezron begot Ram, Ram begot Amminadab, ²⁰Ammina-dab begot Nahshon, Nahshon begot Salmon,ʃ ²¹Salmon begot Boaz, Boaz begot Obed, ²²Obed begot Jesse, and Jesse begot David.

ʃ *Heb. "Salmah."*

The Book of Ruth: A Genealogy

This chart is included as a further guide to help readers understand the genealogy of the characters in the *Book of Ruth*. For reasons of space, it does not include all of the descendents of Abraham and Lot (for example, Jacob's wife Rachel and Jacob's other children are omitted). This chart is based on the following works: *Seder ha-Korot be-Tanakh* (Eliezer Shulman), *Seder ha-Dorot* (Jehiel Heilprin), *Seder Olam Rabbah* (Yosei ben Chalafta), *Pirkei de-Rabbi Eli'ezer* (chapter 11), *Arba'ah Turim* (Ya'akov ben Asher, on *Genesis* 19:26), and *Encyclopedia Otzar Yisra'el* (J. D. Eisenstein, ed.).

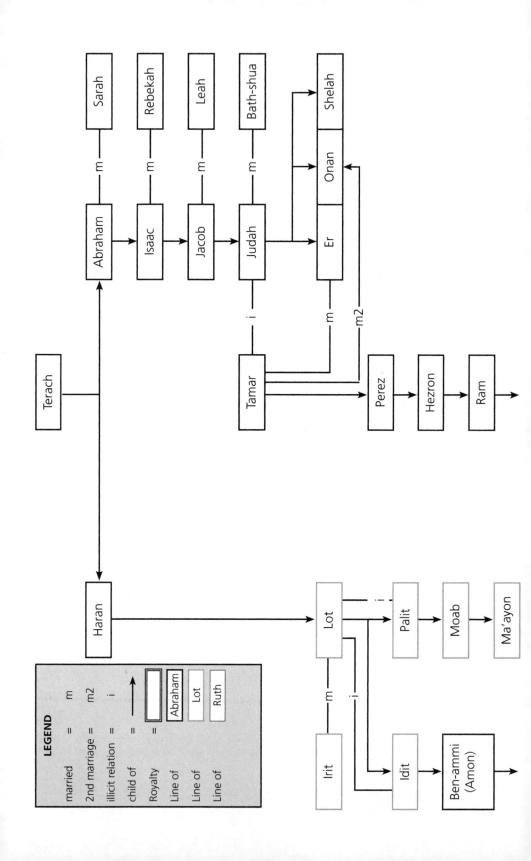

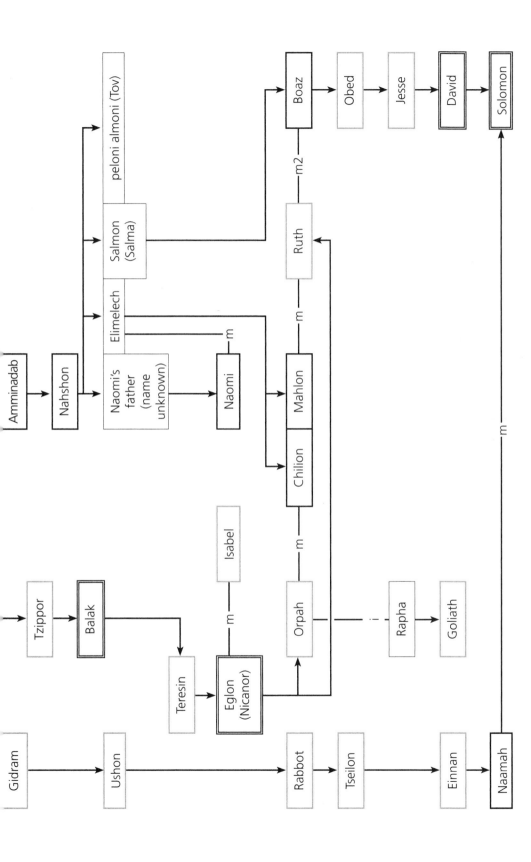

Introductory Questions
on the Book of Ruth

QUESTION: Where in the Bible is the *Book of Ruth* found?

ANSWER: The Jewish Bible consists of three parts:

1. The Pentateuch, or Torah, which is divided into the five books of Moses: *Genesis, Exodus, Leviticus, Numbers,* and *Deuteronomy.*
2. The Prophets, in Hebrew *Nevi'im,* which consists of eight books, including the *Book of Judges* and the *Book of Samuel.*
3. The Writings, in Hebrew *Ketuvim,* which consists of nine books, including the five scrolls, or *megillot,* of which the *Book of Ruth* is one.

The Jewish Bible sometimes is referred to as the Tanakh, an acronym for *Torah, Nevi'im,* and *Ketuvim.*

QUESTION: What are the names of the five *megillot*?

ANSWER: The five scrolls are:

1. *Shir ha-Shirim*—Song of Songs
2. *Rut*—the Book of Ruth
3. *Eikhah*—the Book of Lamentations
4. *Kohelet*—the Book of Ecclesiastes
5. *Ester*—the Book of Esther

———

QUESTION: When do we read each of the five *megillot*?

ANSWER: Each of the five scrolls is associated with a particular Jewish holiday:

1. *Shir ha-Shirim*, known in English as the *Song of Songs*, is read on Passover—Pesach—which commemorates the Exodus from Egypt. Just as the Exodus was an expression of God's love for the Israelites, so, too, does *Shir ha-Shirim* convey God's love for the Jewish people.
2. *Rut*, referred to in English as the *Book of Ruth*, is read during the holiday of Shavuot, which celebrates God's transmission of the written and oral Torah to the Jewish people on Mount Sinai.
3. *Eikhah*, the *Book of Lamentations*, attributed to the prophet Jeremiah, is read on Tishah be-Av, the ninth of the month of Av, which commemorates the destruction of the First and Second Temples in Jerusalem.
4. *Kohelet*, the *Book of Ecclesiastes*, which records the

words of King Solomon and was edited by King Hezekiah, is read on the festival of Sukkot, which follows Rosh Hashanah and Yom Kippur. The narrator of the book, Kohelet, urges us to fulfill God's commandments, an appropriate resolution immediately following the High Holiday period.

5. *Ester*, or the *Book of Esther*, is read on the holiday of Purim and is set in Persia in the fourth century B.C.E. It celebrates the miracle that God performed through Queen Esther and Mordecai by saving the Jewish nation from annihilation at the hands of the evil Haman and the easily duped King Ahasuerus.

QUESTION: Why are these books called "scrolls"?

ANSWER: Before the advent of printing, manuscripts were written by hand on parchment scrolls. Sacred parchments were rolled around wooden rods and unfurled for the purpose of reading. *Megillah* comes from the Hebrew word for "rolling," *galal.* The Torah always is read in the synagogue from a handwritten parchment scroll. In many synagogues the *megillot* also are read from handwritten scrolls.

QUESTION: Must the *megillot* be read from handwritten scrolls?

ANSWER: Although it is preferable, it is not mandatory, except in the case of the *Book of Esther,* which must be read from a handwritten parchment scroll. The other *megillot* may be read from regular printed books.

QUESTION: When does the festival of Shavuot, on which the *Book of Ruth* is read, occur?

ANSWER: The Torah commands that we count seven weeks—forty-nine days—from the second day of Pesach; on the fiftieth day, we celebrate the festival of Shavuot (which literally means "weeks"). The marking off of each of the forty-nine days is called "counting the *omer*." *Omer*, a sheaf of newly harvested barley, refers to the barley offering made in ancient times on the second day of Pesach,[1] the beginning of the grain harvest, which ended on Shavuot.

QUESTION: For how many days is Shavuot observed?

ANSWER: In Israel the holiday is celebrated for one day; in the Diaspora, it is observed for two days.

QUESTION: Why do we observe festivals for two days in the Diaspora?

ANSWER: In ancient times, messengers were sent from Jerusalem to outlying communities to announce the New Moon—the beginning of the new month. With this information, those Jews living outside of the Holy City could calculate the start of each Jewish festival. Because messengers could not always reach these distant communities quickly, however, religious leaders in the Diaspora were unsure about which of two days marked the first day of the new month. To be certain the holidays were celebrated on the correct day, an extra day was added by the Sages to each of the festivals, including at the beginning and end of Sukkot and Pesach, and on Shavuot. Since Rosh Hashanah, the Jewish New Year, falls on the first day of the month, it was difficult to send news of the New Moon to all the Jews of Israel, let alone the Diaspora; therefore, Rosh Hashanah is observed for two days both in- and outside of Israel. The Talmud describes this as a *yoma arikhta*, "a long day." In other words, both days are important.[2] Although astronomical calculations were fixed several centuries ago, the festivals continue to be observed for two days by Jews in the Diaspora out of longstanding tradition. The Yom Kippur fast is observed for one day, both inside and outside of Israel.

——

QUESTION: How does this affect the reading of the *Book of Ruth*?

ANSWER: In the Diaspora, the *Book of Ruth* is read on the second day.

——

QUESTION: When during the Shavuot service is the *Book of Ruth* read?

ANSWER: The *Book of Ruth* is read during the morning service, following the recitation of the Hallel prayer and before the Torah reading.

———

QUESTION: What is Hallel?

ANSWER: The Hallel is a collection of psalms sung in thanksgiving to God in honor of the holidays of Pesach, Shavuot, Sukkot, Rosh Chodesh (the New Month), and Chanukah.

———

QUESTION: What are the two blessings the Sages prescribed to be publicly recited before the reading of the *Book of Ruth*?

ANSWER: The first blessing states that God has commanded us to read the *megillah*. The second blessing, known as She-Hecheyanu, thanks God for keeping us alive, sustaining us, and helping us to reach this special season. These blessings are only recited when the *Book of Ruth* is read from a handwritten parchment scroll, although in some communities it is customary to recite the first blessing even if the *megillah* is read from a printed text.

———

QUESTION: Why is the *Book of Ruth* read on the holiday of Shavuot?

ANSWER: There are several reasons why the *Book of Ruth* is read on Shavuot. First, just as the Jews accepted the Torah given to them by God at Mount Sinai, so did Ruth, born a Moabite, accept the Torah, demonstrating her desire to convert to Judaism at whatever cost to her personal well-being. Second, Ruth was an exemplar of kindness, and the *Book of Ruth* begins and ends with kindness (the story opens with Elimelech, who, before he moved to Moab, was known for his kind deeds; the story closes with Boaz's marriage to Ruth and the birth of their son Obed, for whom Naomi cares), as does the Torah (which opens with God's creation of the world and closes with Moses's burial by God). Third, the *Book of Ruth* is read on Shavuot because it is said that King David, Ruth's great-grandson, was born and died on this date. Since one of the purposes of the *Book of Ruth* was to legitimize David and the Davidic dynasty, what could be more fitting than to read this *megillah* on the day of David's entrance into and departure from this world? The *Book of Ruth* is set during the barley harvest, which also is celebrated on Shavuot. For this reason, too, it is appropriate that we read the *Book of Ruth* as part of the Shavuot festival.

Interestingly, it is said that Rabbi Yisra'el ben Eli'ezer Ba'al Shem Tov—the founder of Chasidism, who often is referred to simply as the Ba'al Shem Tov—died on Shavuot in 1760 (which corresponds to the date 6 Sivan, 5520, on the Jewish calendar).[3] The Ba'al Shem Tov taught that each person could approach God directly,

35

particularly through prayer and the joyous observance of the mitzvot. These teachings reaffirm the messages that are conveyed throughout the *Book of Ruth*.

QUESTION: Who was the author of the *Book of Ruth*?

ANSWER: The *Book of Ruth* traditionally is ascribed to Samuel, the biblical prophet and last of the judges, who lived almost three thousand years ago.[4] Ushering in a new age of prophecy, the Sages refer to Samuel as the "teacher" of all the prophets who followed.[5]

QUESTION: Who was Samuel's mother?

ANSWER: Samuel's mother was Hannah, wife of Elkanah. According to the Sages, she was one of the seven prophetesses of the Bible (the other six are Sarah, Miriam, Deborah, Huldah, Esther, and Abigail).[6] Her devout belief in God and intense prayer merited her a child—Samuel—after many years of barrenness.[7] She vowed to raise her son as a Nazarite (one who did not drink wine or cut his hair) and dedicated him to serve in the sanctuary in Shiloh, in Israel. Perhaps his mother's strength of character and great piety served as an inspiration to Samuel in writing the *Book of Ruth*.

QUESTION: Who was Eli?

ANSWER: Eli served as a judge and, for forty years, as a priest in Shiloh. It was into Eli's care that Hannah delivered her young son Samuel in fulfillment of her vow. Samuel was Eli's foremost disciple, and the two men led the people of Israel during the transition from the era of judges to the era of kings.

———

QUESTION: What other books of the Bible did Samuel write?

ANSWER: Samuel authored the *Book of Judges* and parts of his own book, the *Book of Samuel*.

———

QUESTION: What significant events took place under Samuel's leadership?

ANSWER: It was during Samuel's tenure that the monarchy was instituted in Israel. Samuel anointed Saul as the first king; because of Saul's failure to follow God's orders regarding the destruction of the evil nation of Amalek, he was deemed unworthy. God then instructed Samuel to anoint David as the new king of Israel. The Davidic monarchy would last until the destruction of the First Temple, which occurred in 586 B.C.E. (Some date the destruction of the First Temple to 422 B.C.E., noting a 164–year discrepancy in converting dates from the Hebrew calendar to the secular calendar.) Jewish belief holds that the Messiah will be a descendent of King David.

———

QUESTION: Why did Samuel write the *Book of Ruth*?

ANSWER: Ruth, a Moabite convert to Judaism, was David's great-grandmother. Samuel wrote the *Book of Ruth* in order to substantiate David's God-given claim to the throne of Israel. The *Book of Ruth* is a testament to King David's genealogy as well as his fine character and Ruth's.

———

QUESTION: Why was Ruth's Moabite ancestry problematic?

ANSWER: *Deuteronomy* 23:4 states: "An Ammonite or a Moabite shall not enter into the community of the Lord; even to the tenth generation they shall be prohibited forever from entering the community of the Lord. [This is] because they did not meet you [the Israelites] with bread and with water...when you came out of Egypt, and because they hired Balaam...to curse you." Instead of showing the Israelites compassion by bringing them food and drink when they camped in the plains of Moab after the Exodus from Egypt, the Moabites hired Balaam, a famous sorcerer, to curse them (though he blessed the Israelites instead, predicting that, "A star shall come forth from Jacob and a scepter shall rise out of Israel" [*Numbers* 22–24]). For these reasons, marriages between Jews and Ammonites or Moabites were forbidden, regardless of whether the Ammonite or Moabite converted to Judaism.

QUESTION: If marriages between Jews and Moabites were prohibited, why would Boaz have been permitted to marry Ruth upon the return of Ruth and Naomi to Israel from Moab?

ANSWER: The prohibition applied only to Jewish women who wished to marry Moabite men. Moabite women were permitted to convert to Judaism and marry Israelite men.

QUESTION: Why were Moabite and Ammonite women who converted permitted to marry into the Jewish people?

ANSWER: Moabite and Ammonite *men* were prohibited from joining the Jewish people because of their bad character traits. It would have been the men's responsibility to bring out food and drink to the Israelites passing through Moab after the Exodus from Egypt.

QUESTION: Wouldn't feeding and hosting guests have fallen to the Moabite women?

ANSWER: In ancient times it would have been the women's responsibility to prepare food for guests. However, the onus would have fallen upon the men to serve the guests, particularly if they had to feed the entire Israelite camp.

QUESTION: Is there any evidence in the Bible that Moabite women were really kind?

ANSWER: Ruth the Moabite, a woman of exceptional kindness and humility, which is one of the recurrent themes of the *Book of Ruth*, is the only example of a kind Moabite woman.

QUESTION: Who are the protagonists of the *Book of Ruth*?

ANSWER: The story revolves around two women and one man: Ruth and Naomi, and Boaz.

QUESTION: Who are the other characters in the *Book of Ruth*?

ANSWER: The other characters include Elimelech, Mahlon, Chilion, Orpah, and an unnamed figure referred to only as "so-and-so," in Hebrew *peloni almoni*.

QUESTION: Let's discuss the characters in the *Book of Ruth* in order of their appearance. Who was Elimelech?

ANSWER: The story of *Ruth* opens with Elimelech, husband of Naomi and father of Mahlon and Chilion. A leader from the tribe of Judah of great stature and wealth, Elimelech was a pillar of kindness, always ready to help a fellow Israelite[8]—until famine struck Canaan. Though he could have survived the calamity, he closed his heart to his fellow Israelites and fled to enemy territory: Moab. There he lost his fortune and then his life.

———

QUESTION: Who was Naomi?

ANSWER: Naomi was Elimelech's wife, the mother of Mahlon and Chilion, and the mother-in-law of Ruth and Orpah. Naomi left the land of Israel a wealthy and respected woman, only to return a destitute widow.

———

QUESTION: Who were Mahlon and Chilion?

ANSWER: Mahlon and Chilion were the sons of Elimelech and Naomi. They accompanied their parents to Moab. Upon Elimelech's death, they married non-Jewish—Moabite—women. Mahlon married Ruth; Chilion, Orpah. About ten years after moving to Moab, the brothers died penniless and without children.

———

QUESTION: Who was Ruth?

ANSWER: Ruth, the heroine of our story, was, according to the Midrash, of royal descent, daughter of King Eglon of Moab.[9] Married to Mahlon, son of Elimelech and Naomi, Ruth converted to Judaism upon her husband's death and accompanied her mother-in-law from Moab to Bethlehem, uttering the famous words, "[W]herever you go, I will go; wherever you lodge, I will lodge; your people shall be my people, and your God my God" (*Ruth* 1:16).

————

QUESTION: Who was Orpah?

ANSWER: Like Ruth, Orpah also was a daughter of King Eglon of Moab.[10] Orpah married Mahlon's brother, Chilion, but upon his death was persuaded by Naomi to return to her family.

————

QUESTION: Who was Boaz?

ANSWER: Boaz, Elimelech's nephew,[11] was "a man of substance" (2:1) and is the hero of our story. It was Boaz who would redeem Elimelech's property and marry Ruth. Ruth and Boaz's son, Obed, was King David's grandfather.

————

QUESTION: Who was *peloni almoni*?

ANSWER: *Peloni almoni*, which is the Hebrew equivalent of "so-and-so," was, according to the Midrash, Elimelech's brother.[12] *Peloni almoni* had what we would call today "the right of first refusal," the right—over Boaz—to redeem Elimelech's property and marry Ruth. Already married and concerned about imperiling his children's inheritance, *peloni almoni* declined.

————

QUESTION: According to the Sages, Ruth lived to a very old age, meriting to see the building of the First Temple by her great-great-grandson, King Solomon. Where is Ruth buried?

ANSWER: Although the archaeological evidence is inconclusive, some contemporary religious experts believe that Ruth is buried in Admot Yishai, near the city of Hebron, which is one of the world's oldest cities and the site of the cave of Machpelah, where the patriarchs and matriarchs Abraham and Sarah, Isaac and Rebekah, and Jacob and Leah are buried. Fittingly, Hebron was King David's original royal city. Today, some people make pilgrimages to what is believed to be Ruth's grave.

Chapter 1

Synopsis

Over three thousand years ago lived a man named Elimelech, a highly esteemed citizen of Bethlehem in Israel, owner of livestock and abundant tracts of farmland. When famine swept the country, he and his wife, Naomi, and their two sons, Mahlon and Chilion, fled to the land of Moab, despite the hostility of the Moabite people toward the Israelite nation.

Elimelech soon died, and Mahlon and Chilion married Moabite women, in defiance of the biblical law prohibiting such a union. Ten years later, both sons perished, leaving their grieving, childless wives, Ruth and Orpah, and their widowed mother destitute.

Ruth and Orpah clung steadfastly to Naomi. When Naomi learned from traveling merchants that the famine in Judea had come to an end, she decided to return to Bethlehem. In spite of Naomi's attempts to dissuade them, both daughters-in-law insisted on setting out toward Judea with Naomi. Early along the journey, Naomi convinced Orpah to return to the comforts of Moab. Ruth, however, had decided that she wanted to become a member of the Jewish people and accompanied Naomi all the way to Bethlehem, where they were greeted by the surprised townspeople.

——

QUESTION: The first word of the *Book of Ruth* is *vayehi*, "there was" or "it was," which is repeated four words later. What is the significance of this word and its repetition?

ANSWER: In Hebrew, the first part of the word *vayehi* is *vay*, which means "alas!" or "woe!" This, of course, is quite similar to an expression we're all familiar with: "oy vay!" The repetition of the word, the Sages tell us, foreshadows the sad events that are about to be described.[1]

——

QUESTION: The first verse of the *Book of Ruth* tells us that the story is set in the time of the chieftans or judges. Why is this important to our understanding of the story?

ANSWER: The *Book of Ruth* begins during a period of famine. Elimelech abandons his fellow Jews and leaves Israel for Moab with his wife and sons. By telling us that this action occurred during the time of the judges, we can place the story in context. At this period in Jewish history, there was not yet a king or central authority to supervise the Israelites; thus, Elimelech could not be prevented from leaving the land of Israel and moving to Moab. As the last line of the *Book of Judges* (21:25) reads,

"In those days there was no king in Israel; every man did what was right in his own eyes."

———

QUESTION: The first verse is even more specific. It tells us that the story takes place *bimei shefot ha-shoftim*, "In the days when the judges were judging." Isn't it obvious that judges judge? Wouldn't it have been simpler to write: "during the epoch of the judges"?

ANSWER: The expression "the judges were judging" can be understood to mean that the judges were being judged. Instead of effectively leading the Israelites, some judges were inept—unable to influence men like Elimelech to do the right thing and remain in Israel—or even corrupt, accepting bribes in payment for favorable rulings.

———

QUESTION: Is there another explanation for the phrase *shefot ha-shoftim*?

ANSWER: Some interpret the verse to mean that God, Himself, judged the judges.[2] Because they and their fellow Israelites were corrupt, a divinely decreed famine struck the land of Israel.

———

QUESTION: Are there other interpretations?

ANSWER: Yes. On a more positive note some commentators explain the phrase to mean, "during the time of the judge among judges," referring to Boaz.[3]

QUESTION: Why would Boaz have been thought of as a "judge among judges"?

ANSWER: God was about to send a famine to punish the Israelites for their sins. Yet even when God punishes His people, He shows them compassion. He wanted to be sure that they would have someone to pray for them, to give them support, and to help them keep the faith, so He waited until the Israelites were led by a special judge, a judge among judges—Boaz.

QUESTION: Why was Boaz's name not explicitly mentioned in the first verse of the *Book of Ruth*?

ANSWER: Elimelech was Boaz's uncle. His conduct was extremely embarrassing to Boaz. The *Book of Ruth* tries to mute this embarrassing detail by not mentioning Boaz's name.

QUESTION: What was life like during the time of the judges?

ANSWER: After Joshua, the leader who followed Moses, died, the era of the judges began. It was characterized by a lack of central leadership and a lack of cohesion among the tribes. Although most of the land of Israel had been conquered and shared equitably among the various tribes of Israel, the Israelites failed to scrupulously obey the Torah and strayed into idolatry. As a result, they lost God's divine protection and fell into the hands of various enemies, including the Philistines, Canaanites, and Midianites. But strong leaders also emerged, who helped unify Israel and defeat Israel's enemies, and who encouraged the Israelites to abandon their sinful ways and return with full hearts to God. These individuals were the judges, and included such men and women as Othniel, Ehud, Deborah, Gideon, Jephthah, and Samson.

———

QUESTION: Verse 1 says, "There was a famine in the land." Was this the first famine ever to occur in Israel?

ANSWER: No. Several famines had already struck the land. In the earliest period of Jewish history, God commanded our patriarch Abraham to leave his home and travel to Canaan. No sooner had he arrived in Canaan than a famine descended upon the land, a test by God of Abraham's belief in Him. Unshakable in his faith, Abraham sojourned in Egypt until the crisis had passed (*Genesis* 12).

———

QUESTION: What other famines occurred in the land of Israel?

ANSWER: According to the Sages, ten terrible famines would befall the world before the coming of the Messiah. Nine of these famines have already occurred, the famine recorded in the *Book of Ruth* having been the sixth. They took place during the days of:

1. Adam, the first human being
2. Lamech, the father of Noah
3. the patriarch Abraham
4. the patriarch Isaac
5. the patriarch Jacob
6. Boaz
7. King David
8. the prophet Elijah
9. the prophet Elisha

The final famine, it is said, will precede the Messianic era. People will hunger neither for bread nor water. They will thirst only for the word of God.[4]

———

QUESTION: Is there a difference between famine in the land of Israel and famine elsewhere?

ANSWER: God says in *Deuteronomy* 11:10–12 that the land of Israel is special: "It is a land that the Lord your God is concerned about; the eyes of the Lord your God are always upon it, from the beginning of the year until the end of the year." According to the Sages, a famine in the land of Israel is a direct manifestation of God's anger toward His people.[5]

QUESTION: Was the famine we read about in the *Book of Ruth* restricted to the land of Israel or were neighboring countries also affected?

ANSWER: Only in the land of Israel was there famine, a punishment sent by God to the Jewish people. Elimelech went to Moab, where there was no lack of food.

QUESTION: The first verse of *Ruth* seems to link the occurrence of the famine to the behavior of the judges. Is there a connection?

ANSWER: The judges were the leaders of their day. Even if the people had sinned, their leaders had the power to protect them. The judges, however, were not influential enough to avert God's harsh decree. They, themselves, must have sinned in some way and thus also were responsible for the famine.

QUESTION: Are there other examples in the Torah of those who failed to lead and who provoked God's wrath?

ANSWER: Yes, there are many. One of the most familiar stories is that of Sodom and Gomorrah. Abraham pleaded with God to spare these cities of sin if only ten righteous individuals could be found in their midst. Not even ten righteous people could be found, however, and the cities and their inhabitants were destroyed (*Genesis* 18–19).

———

QUESTION: Where in the Bible do we find an example of a leader who prevented the downfall of his nation?

ANSWER: God freed the Israelites from slavery in Egypt, saved them from the Egyptian army at the Red Sea, provided food and water for them in the desert, and gave them the Torah. Yet when the Israelites, panicked by Moses's prolonged, forty-day absence on Mount Sinai, fashioned a golden calf to worship, God threatened to destroy the Israelites and make Moses the leader of a new nation. Moses begged God to spare the Jews: "Do not be angry at the people whom you took out of the land of Egypt . . . Don't let the Egyptians say '. . . He delivered them [from bondage] only to kill them . . .'" (*Exodus* 32:11–12). Had not Moses interceded on the Israelites' behalf—just one of many times that he did so—God would have annihilated them.

———

QUESTION: In the first verse of *Ruth*, Elimelech is referred to as an *ish* of Bethlehem. What does *ish* mean and why is this word used?

ANSWER: *Ish* is the Hebrew word for "man"; its use in the Torah always indicates a VIP—a highly esteemed individual of good upbringing. For example, the word *ish* is used to refer to Moses when he took Zipporah as his wife (*Exodus* 2:20), and it also is used to describe Moses's father-in-law, Jethro (*Exodus* 2:21), who granted Moses sanctuary when he fled Egypt after killing an Egyptian taskmaster and who offered Moses sage advice about the appointment of judges.

——

QUESTION: How important a man was Elimelech?

ANSWER: Elimelech, member of the illustrious tribe of Judah, was the son of Nahshon. Pursued by the Egyptian army following the Exodus, Nahshon, the Sages tell us,[6] was the first to jump into the Red Sea, showing his complete faith in God that the waters would part and the Israelites would be able to walk through on dry land (*Exodus* 14). Perhaps the most prominent citizen of Bethlehem, Elimelech was an extremely wealthy individual who always put the needs of his brethren above his own. When faced with the most difficult test—in this case, famine in the land of Israel—Elimelech failed and abandoned his people to go to Moab. His sin was regarded not just as personal wrongdoing but as tantamount to treason.

——

QUESTION: What does the name Elimelech mean?

ANSWER: *Eli* means "my God" and reflects the side of Elimelech that was godly and humble. *Melekh* means "king," and indeed, Elimelech had a royal aura. A prince among men, a born leader, a man possessing great spiritual and material wealth, Elimelech unfortunately lacked the moral resources to endure the test presented by famine in the land of Canaan.

———

QUESTION: Why was Bethlehem such an important city?

ANSWER: Bethlehem—in Hebrew, Beit Lechem—means "house of bread." This implies that the city was a prosperous one, well placed and strategically and symbolically important. In *Genesis* 35:19 we are told that the matriarch Rachel died giving birth to Benjamin in Bethlehem and was buried there. Bethlehem is a place close to the heart and soul of the Jewish people; to this day, Kever Rachel, Rachel's Tomb, is a holy site to which many Jews journey to pray.

———

QUESTION: What was significant about the tribe of Judah?

ANSWER: Our forefather Jacob, son of Isaac and grandson of Abraham, the first Jew, had twelve children. Although Reuben was the oldest, it was Judah who received a special blessing from his father: "The scepter shall not depart from Judah, nor the ruler's staff from between his feet" (*Genesis* 49:10). In other words, the future leaders of the Jewish people would come from the tribe of Judah. As a member of the tribe of Judah, Elimelech was held in high regard by his fellow citizens. When he left Bethlehem for Moab, the townspeople felt betrayed and abandoned; he had dealt them a terrible blow. It would take Boaz, also a leader of Judah, to repair the damage that Elimelech had done.

——

QUESTION: Why would a role model like Elimelech—a community leader, a judge, and a philanthropist—just pick up and leave his hometown?

ANSWER: Elimelech's actions defy logic. But on a mystical level, one can say that he was dispatched by God on a mission to redeem Ruth. [7]

——

QUESTION: Had Elimelech remained in Israel, how might things have been different?

ANSWER: Had Elimelech stayed in Bethlehem with his wife and sons, rather than fleeing to Moab, his very presence might have given his fellow Israelites strength and courage. Elimelech could have prayed to God to stop the famine, to bring rain, and to restore the harvest. He and his sons might not have died premature deaths.

——

QUESTION: Why did Elimelech choose to go to Moab rather than any of the other countries surrounding Israel?

ANSWER: Elimelech was a miser. He was unwilling to risk his fortune to aid his neighbors during the famine. Attracted to Moab like a magnet, Elimelech ran away from his people, his land, and his destiny to join a nation known for *their* stinginess. The Torah curses the people of Moab for failing to share even bread and water with the Israelites following the Exodus. Ruth, on the other hand, rejected the country of her birth and eagerly joined the Israelite nation.

———

QUESTION: How did Elimelech die?

ANSWER: Poverty, says the Talmud, is worse than death.[8] Elimelech died twice, first when he lost all of his money, then when he lost his life. God often diminishes a person gradually, giving him or her a chance to repent. But though he lost his fortune, Elimelech failed to correct his evil ways.

———

QUESTION: Naomi was Elimelech's wife and the mother of Mahlon and Chilion. What does the name Naomi mean?

ANSWER: The name Naomi comes from the root *na'am*, meaning "pleasant." Naomi was a pleasant, exceptionally refined woman. However, because of all the tragedies that had befallen her—the death of her husband and sons—she asked not to be called Naomi anymore, but Mara, meaning "bitter," for God had made her life bitter (1:20).

QUESTION: Were Naomi and Elimelech related only by marriage?

ANSWER: No. According to the Midrash, Naomi was Elimelech's niece.[9]

QUESTION: Was Naomi willing to go to Moab, or did she protest Elimelech's decision to leave Bethlehem?

ANSWER: The Midrash says that Naomi was good-natured and sweet, following her husband to Moab out of wifely loyalty.[10] Unlike Sarah, wife of Abraham, who often spoke her mind, Naomi was passive and obedient. Mahlon and Chilion, too, deferred to Elimelech's decision to move to Moab.

QUESTION: Could Naomi have refused to go to Moab with Elimelech?

ANSWER: One should never underestimate the power of a wife. Had she tried, she might have been able to persuade Elimelech to remain in Bethlehem, saving his life and the lives of their sons. Even had Elimelech insisted on leaving, he could not have forced her to go with him. Some Sages believe, however, that Naomi also wanted to escape the famine in Bethlehem.[11]

QUESTION: Is there any other indication that Naomi was untroubled about leaving Bethlehem?

ANSWER: Yes. Had Naomi left the land of Israel only because she felt obligated to follow her husband, she would have returned immediately upon his death. However, she remained in Moab with her sons for the next decade.

QUESTION: Whose wife *did* save her husband from sinning?

ANSWER: *Numbers* 16 describes how Korah and 250 followers waged a bitter rebellion against Moses in the wilderness. Among the rebels was a man named On, son of Peleth, from the tribe of Reuben. According to the Midrash, On's wife realized how misguided the rebels were and worked hard to convince her husband to abandon the fight. Afraid for his life, On did not know how to disassociate himself from Korah. Warning On to remain inside their tent, his wife sat at the entrance combing her hair. As long as her hair was unbound, Korah did not dare approach. On's wife maintained her vigil at the entrance to her tent until Korah gave up. Later that very day, Korah and his followers were swallowed up by the earth for their sins. On was spared.[12]

QUESTION: How old were Naomi's sons Mahlon and Chilion when they left Bethlehem?

ANSWER: The Sages say that Mahlon and Chilion were twelve and seventeen years old, respectively, when they accompanied their parents to Moab.[13]

QUESTION: From where does the name Mahlon come?

ANSWER: Mahlon comes from the Hebrew word *machalah*, which means "sickness." Indeed, Mahlon's actions greatly displeased God, who brought down upon him sickness and finally death.

QUESTION: From where does the name Chilion come?

ANSWER: The Hebrew word *kilayon*, from which Chilion's name comes, means "destruction" or "annihilation." Unlike Ruth, Orpah, wife of Mahlon's brother Chilion, did not convert to Judaism, and instead of accompanying Naomi and Ruth to the land of Israel, she returned to her people and their idolatrous ways. It is said that Goliath, the great Philistine warrior whom

King David slew with a slingshot, is descended from Orpah.[14] We conclude from this that Chilion's sin was not forgiven.

———

QUESTION: Are the derivations of the names Mahlon and Chilion open to other interpretations?

ANSWER: Knowing as we do of the sins of Mahlon and Chilion, we tend to focus on the negative words from which their names are derived. However, the Sages teach us that when Mahlon and Chilion were born to Elimelech and Naomi, their parents looked to the future with hope.[15] The name Mahlon may be related to the word *machal*, which means "pardon" or "forgive." Although Mahlon sinned gravely and died because of it, God finally forgave him. Ruth's marriage to Boaz assured not only that Elimelech's property would remain in the family, but that the family's name would be carried on. Thus, through the deeds of his virtuous wife, Ruth, Mahlon was redeemed. Chilion's name may come from the Hebrew word *kol*, which literally means "all" but metaphorically means the "world," as in *tikkun olam,* "repairing the world" through acts of loving-kindness.

———

QUESTION: Other Sages identify Mahlon and Chilion with Joash and Saraph of *1 Chronicles* 4:22. What do the names Joash and Saraph mean?

ANSWER: According to the Talmud, Mahlon and Chilion were originally named Joash and Saraph, respectively, names with positive connotations.[16] *Yoash* is derived from two Hebrew words, the first, spelled *yod-he*, meaning "God," and the second, *aish*, meaning "fire"; *saraf* is a Hebrew word meaning "burn." Both names conjure images of God's holy fire. However, after Elimelech and Naomi's sons sinned, the names Joash and Saraph were interpreted negatively: Yoash, from the Hebrew word *ye'ush*, which means to "despair" or "lose hope," signifying that Mahlon lost his chance for future redemption; and Saraph, referring to God's "fire" as in "wrath." The Talmud says that Mahlon, instead of repenting when he became ill, "took his body and made it worthless," meaning that he had forbidden relationships. Through Mahlon and Chilion, the prophet Samuel conveyed the dangers of disobeying God and incurring His wrath.

QUESTION: Why, upon mention of Elimelech's death in verse 3, is he referred to as "Elimelech, Naomi's husband," when verse 2 has already made clear that Naomi was Elimelech's wife?

ANSWER: Elimelech was a virtuous, righteous man during the first part of his life; it wasn't until his latter years that he sinned. Naomi, in contrast, was free of sin all her life. Samuel, the author of the *Book of Ruth*, was always protective of the reputations of his subjects.

Therefore, he tried to invest Elimelech with some of Naomi's goodness by referring to him as her husband. This is consistent with Jewish tradition, which cautions against speaking ill of the dead.

———

QUESTION: Why else is Elimelech referred to as "Elimelech, Naomi's husband"?

ANSWER: The Talmud draws an important lesson from this.[17] When a woman's husband (or a man's wife) dies, friends will grieve the passing of a dear companion, but their lives will continue basically unchanged. Even children, following the death of a parent, will build lives of their own. A wife's life, however, is usually turned upside down with the passing of her husband. Her pain and grief are greater than anybody else's. Verse 3 of *Ruth* teaches that Naomi remained faithful to the memory of her husband and did not remarry—in other words, Elimelech remained "Naomi's husband."

———

QUESTION: Mahlon and Chilion married Ruth and Orpah (1:4), said to be the daughters of King Eglon of Moab. Did the women share the same mother?

ANSWER: Most Sages agree that they did.[18] Some contend that Ruth and Orpah were only half sisters—they shared the same father but had different mothers; this is based on *Ruth* 1:8, which says, "Turn back, each of you to her mother's house."

———

QUESTION: What attracted Mahlon and Chilion to Ruth and Orpah?

ANSWER: The Sages say that upon the death of their father, Mahlon and Chilion, uncertain about their future prospects, eagerly married Ruth and Orpah, daughters of Eglon.[19]

———

QUESTION: How did Ruth and Orpah's father, King Eglon, die?

ANSWER: King Eglon was a tyrannical leader who attacked the land of Israel and subjugated its inhabitants for eighteen years, until he was assassinated by Ehud, son of Gera, a Jew. Ehud presented the king with a basket of gifts and later snuck back to the palace, where he killed the obese Eglon with a dagger hidden beneath his cloak (*Judges* 3). Eglon's assassination took place before Mahlon and Chilion married Ruth and Orpah.

———

QUESTION: How did such a righteous woman— Ruth—come from such a wicked father?

ANSWER: According to the Kabbalah, the Jewish mystical tradition, Ruth was a reincarnation of Lot, Abraham's nephew, whom Abraham treated like a son.[20] Though Lot lived among the depraved citizens of Sodom, he had learned about kindness from Abraham. Thus, say the mystics, Ruth's soul redeemed Lot's. This ties in nicely with the tradition that a convert to Judaism, as Ruth was, is considered a newborn child and called the son or daughter of Abraham (in fact, male converts usually take the Hebrew name Abraham and female converts the Hebrew name Ruth). Other Sages say that because Eglon stood when Ehud told the king that he had a message for him from God, Eglon merited Ruth's salvation.[21]

———

QUESTION: What does the name Ruth mean?

ANSWER: It is said that Ruth's name at birth was Gi-lit.[22] According to the Midrash, the name Ruth comes from the word *revayah*, which means "abundance" or "satura-tion"[23]; King David, Ruth's great-grandson, filled the world with his beautiful psalms praising God, like someone who waters a dry field and makes it bloom. When one adds together the numerical value of each of the letters of Ruth's name (this system is called *gimatriyyah*, and yields fasci-nating insights and interpretations)—*raish, vav, tav*—they total 606 (*raish* equals 200; *vav*, 6; and *tav*, 400). The To-rah contains 613 laws. If we subtract the seven Noahic laws (see below), which all people, not just Jews, are com-manded to obey, there remain 606 laws reserved for the Jewish people. The minute Ruth became a convert, she embraced the Torah, taking upon herself those additional 606 commandments. Even numerically she was a role model! According to the Talmud, she lived such a long life that she saw her great-grandson become king.

———

QUESTION: What are the seven Noahic laws that were given by God to Noah and, by extension, to all mankind?

ANSWER: The seven Noahic laws prohibit idolatry, blasphemy, murder, sexual immorality, robbery, and eating the limb of a living creature, and require the establishment of courts of justice.[24]

QUESTION: What does the name Orpah mean?

ANSWER: The name Orpah comes from the Hebrew word *oref*, which means "nape of the neck." What a fitting name for a woman who turned her back on Judaism and reverted to a life of idolatry.

QUESTION: Did Ruth and Orpah convert to Judaism before they married Mahlon and Chilion?

ANSWER: The majority of Sages say that they did not convert to Judaism before marrying Naomi's sons—which is why Mahlon and Chilion were punished by death. Some commentators contend that the two women told their husbands they would convert but were not sincere. Other scholars say the sisters were too young at the time of their marriage to make a binding commitment to convert.[25]

QUESTION: How did Naomi react to her sons marrying Moabite women?

ANSWER: Naomi is said to have been a devoted mother; some Sages, however, fault her for her passivity, for failing to prevent her sons from marrying Moabite women. Other Sages argue that Naomi was very upset but "kept silent and held her intense pain in check." That could very well be the case since she left Moab as soon as her sons died, though they and their father were all buried in Moab.[26]

———

QUESTION: How long were Naomi's sons married before they died?

ANSWER: Verse 4 of the *Book of Ruth* tells us that they were married for about ten years.

———

QUESTION: What is significant about the number ten?

ANSWER: The Sages teach that if a couple is married for ten years without producing children, the husband may divorce his wife.[27] Indeed, the patriarch Abraham and the matriarch Sarah lived in Canaan—the Promised Land—for ten years without having children. That is why Sarah gave Abraham her handmaid, Hagar, in the hope that Hagar would produce an heir for Abraham (which she did, Ishmael; *Genesis* 16:3).

Likewise, Isaac and his wife, Rebekah, were child-less—for twenty years. According to the Midrash, Re-bekah was too young during the first ten years of their marriage to bear children, so those years are discounted. Ten years later, when Isaac might have considered tak-ing another wife, he and Rebekah merited to have chil-dren together. God accepted their prayers, and the twins Jacob and Esau were born (*Genesis* 25:21).

―――

QUESTION: The Sages teach us that God punished Mahlon and Chilion for marrying Moabite women.[28] Why else did God punish them?

ANSWER: Unlike Elimelech, who was punished by God for leaving Israel during the time of famine, Mahlon and Chilion were punished for failing to return to Is-rael immediately after the death of their father.[29] Instead, they married Moabite women and remained in Moab until God took their lives.

―――

QUESTION: Why did God wait ten years before pun-ishing Mahlon and Chilion?

ANSWER: God is compassionate and gives sinners ample time to repent. Unfortunately, Mahlon and Chil-ion did not take advantage of the opportunity God gave them. Like their father, Elimelech, they first lost all their money.[30] This should have made them realize that they were being punished for their wrongdoing. But Mahlon and Chilion were completely blind to their transgressions and paid in the end with their lives.

———

QUESTION: Naomi was grief-stricken by Elimelech's death. How did she feel when her sons, Mahlon and Chilion, died?

ANSWER: Naomi's devastation must have been profound. The deaths of Mahlon and Chilion left her frightened and brokenhearted; her entire support network was back in Israel—if it still existed, because many years had passed since she had left Israel. She was now an older, frailer woman with increasing fears about aging, loneliness, and financial matters.

———

QUESTION: Verse 6 says that Naomi started out with her daughters-in-law to return from Moab to the land of Israel. What made Naomi decide to go back to her homeland?

ANSWER: Naomi learned that the famine had ended in the Holy Land and resolved to leave the ill-fated Moab, where she had known nothing but grief. She planned to leave immediately after observing the seven-day mourning period—known as *shivah*—for her sons.[31] Had she stayed in Moab, she felt sure she would die an early death, too.

———

QUESTION: How did Naomi learn that the famine had ended in Israel and that the economic picture had improved?

ANSWER: One source says that Jewish peddlers came to Moab selling the produce of the Holy Land.[32] It was from these peddlers that Naomi heard the good news that the famine was over.

———

QUESTION: Was Naomi fearful of the reception she would receive from the townspeople of Bethlehem upon her return home?

ANSWER: Bethlehem was the city of Naomi's youth; she felt called to return. The Torah commands Jews to care for the poor and to show compassion for the needy. Naomi believed deeply in the goodness of the people of Israel and was confident of their loving nature and their ability to forgive.

———

QUESTION: Naomi urged her daughters-in-law, "Turn back, each of you to her mother's house. May the Lord deal kindly with you, as you have dealt with the dead and with me" (1:8). Why does Naomi exhort her daughters-in-law to return to their mothers' houses rather than their father's house?

ANSWER: The Torah tells us that Eliezer, Abraham's trusted servant, went to Haran to find a bride for Isaac,

Abraham's son (*Genesis* 24). Through God's miraculous intervention, Eliezer recognized Rebekah as being the perfect spouse for Isaac. Eliezer gave Rebekah the beautiful jewelry he had taken along and asked her if it would be possible for him to spend the night in her home. She answered affirmatively, and then, the Torah tells us, she "ran and told her mother's household" (*Genesis* 24:28) all that had transpired. The great eleventh-century commentator Rashi (an acronym for Rabbi Shelomoh Yitzchaki), remarks that in those times the women had their own quarters, where they worked and spent their days. A daughter, being especially close to her mother, would go to her, rather than her father, with important news. That is why Rebekah went to her mother's household.

The same is true in our story. Naomi understood the privileged mother-daughter relationship. When trying to persuade Ruth and Orpah to return home rather than accompany her to Israel, Naomi's mention of their "mother's house" evokes vivid memories of a cherished place. She appreciated Ruth and Orpah's loyalty to her: though their husbands were dead, they would not abandon her. Nevertheless, Naomi reminded them, "I'm only the mother of your deceased husbands. Why not return where your heart really belongs, to your own mothers?"

———

QUESTION: Why does Naomi invoke the dead before the living in verse 8: "...May the Lord deal kindly with you, as you have dealt with the dead and with me"?

ANSWER: The Midrash remarks on the great kindness Ruth and Orpah showed their mother-in-law in laying Mahlon and Chilion to rest.[33] According to Moabite law, a man was required to set aside money to cover his burial expenses and to sustain his widow after his death. In the event that he died penniless, his family was obligated to assume those responsibilities. When Mahlon and Chilion died, Naomi couldn't even afford the shrouds in which to wrap them. Ruth and Orpah, however, somehow found the money to give their husbands a proper burial. This is to what Naomi refers when she asks God to repay Ruth and Orpah for their kindness to the dead. Naomi and Orpah also were entitled to money for their living expenses. Naomi would have been obligated to pay them, but in their great kindness, Ruth and Orpah waived any such claim. Naomi asked God to reward them for this, as well.

———

QUESTION: Instead of agreeing to return to their own homes, Ruth and Orpah replied to Naomi, "No, we will return with you to your people" (1:10). Why "your people" and not "our people"?

ANSWER: Ruth and Orpah intended to accompany Naomi to the land of Israel. However, they did not plan to convert to Judaism, which is why they referred to "your people" and not "our people."

———

QUESTION: "Why should you go with me?" Naomi asked her daughters-in-law (1:11). "Have I any more sons in my body who might be husbands for you?" What did Naomi mean?

ANSWER: Naomi's response to her daughters-in-law was rhetorical. She had no plans to remarry and probably was past her childbearing years. But even if Naomi were to have sons in the future, by whom Ruth and Orpah could have sons to carry on their deceased husbands' names, they, too would have been well past their childbearing years by the time Naomi's baby boys were old enough to marry.

QUESTION: If Naomi was too old to bear more children, why couldn't she help Ruth and Orpah find other Jewish men to marry in Israel?

ANSWER: If Ruth and Orpah were unwilling to convert to Judaism, Naomi believed it impossible for her daughters-in-law to find husbands in Israel. Without converting to Judaism, Naomi knew that no Israelite man would marry Ruth or Orpah.

QUESTION: Orpah decided to return home. She "... kissed her mother-in-law farewell. But Ruth clung to [Naomi]" (1:14). What is the difference between these two signs of affection, kissing and clinging?

ANSWER: Orpah never intended to convert to Judaism: she genuinely desired to remain with her mother-in-law, for Orpah could sense the greatness and holiness of the nation of Israel, but she wasn't ready to embrace Jewish practice. Naomi convinced her that it would be too difficult for her to live as a foreigner in Israel. Orpah gave her mother-in-law a parting kiss and left. (Interestingly, Orpah did not kiss Ruth goodbye. Perhaps she sensed that they were already a world apart.) Ruth, on the other hand, clung to her mother-in-law out of enormous love for her but also for all of Judaism; she *was* prepared to embrace the Jewish religion. Had Naomi not taken Ruth to Israel with her, Ruth would have made the journey on her own. Luckily, Naomi recognized the depth of Ruth's feelings. Orpah's kiss expressed love, but Ruth's gesture was more intense and passionate.

QUESTION: What happened to Orpah on her way home?

ANSWER: According to the Sages, after leaving Naomi and Ruth, Orpah was attacked by a gang of men and brutally raped.[34] She became pregnant and gave birth to Goliath, who would become King Saul's archenemy and whom David would slay with a slingshot (*1 Samuel* 17).

QUESTION: Why did such a terrible fate befall Orpah?

ANSWER: Perhaps Orpah's initial offer to accompany Naomi to the Holy Land was insincere. Even if she hadn't converted, Orpah could have lived a virtuous life among the people of Israel, yet she chose to remain among the evil Moabites.[35]

———

QUESTION: Was Orpah rewarded in any way for accompanying Naomi even a short distance on her journey?

ANSWER: Certainly. It is said that God rewards every good deed, every step in the right direction, no matter how small.

———

QUESTION: How was Orpah rewarded?

ANSWER: Our Sages say that Orpah accompanied Naomi for forty steps. Therefore, Goliath, her son, stood against the Israelites for forty days (*1 Samuel* 17:16) before being defeated by David.[36]

———

QUESTION: What convinced Naomi that Ruth was sincere in her desire to convert to Judaism?

ANSWER: Elimelech, Mahlon, and Chilion had left Naomi and her daughters-in-law destitute. Naomi was far too old to bear additional sons for Ruth and Orpah to someday marry. Naomi also may have been apprehensive about the welcome she would receive from the townspeople when she returned to Bethlehem. Her message to Ruth was clear: "I have nothing to offer you. Cast your lot with me and you will have to bear not only personal suffering and hardship, but the suffering and hardships of the entire Jewish nation! Becoming a Jew requires a total commitment to Jewish laws, values, and traditions." Yet knowing this, Ruth persisted: "Do not urge me to leave you....For wherever you go, I will go; wherever you lodge, I will lodge; your people shall be my people, and your God my God..." (1:16).[37]

QUESTION: Where in the Torah do we learn about insincere converts to Judaism? What were the consequences?

ANSWER: When the Jews were freed from bondage in Egypt, the Torah tells us that many Egyptians left with them and converted to Judaism.[38] Some of these Egyptians were sincere about converting; others joined the Jewish nation to improve their standard of living. According to a number of biblical commentators, many of these Egyptians found Jewish observance too difficult. The converts became bitter and resentful, and rebelled.[39] They instigated the building of the golden calf, a sin for which the entire Jewish nation was almost wiped out by God (only Moses's pleas spared the Jews). For this reason, Jews do not actively seek converts.

QUESTION: Are there other examples of insincere converts to Judaism?

ANSWER: Yes. When Joshua began the Jewish conquest of the Land of Israel, the native Canaanites were terrified. The residents of one town, the Gibeonites, disguised themselves as dusty travelers from a distant land who wanted to convert to Judaism. Joshua made a pact with them, but when he learned they were insincere about converting and only cared about saving their lives, he decreed that from that day forward they would never be more than wood choppers and water drawers (*Joshua 9*).

———

QUESTION: Who were the Samaritans?

ANSWER: The Samaritans, or Cutheans as they were known in the Talmud[40] (in Hebrew they are called Kutim), also were considered insincere converts to Judaism. After the mass exile of Israelites to Assyria in the eighth century B.C.E., the Assyrians brought foreign settlers into Samaria—including people from Cuthah—to take the place of the exiled Jews. Because the Kutim did not worship God, God sent lions to terrorize and kill them. Out of fear, the Cutheans brought back one of the exiled Jewish priests to teach them the laws of their new land, and they converted en masse to Judaism. Nevertheless, they continued to worship their idols and were not permitted by the Jewish community to help rebuild the Temple. The Samaritans built their own temple on Mount Gerizim. Pockets of Samaritans exist today, and though their temple was destroyed centuries ago, Mount Gerizim remains the focal point of Samaritan worship.

QUESTION: The difficulty of insincere converts aside, why else does Judaism discourage converts?

ANSWER: Conversion to Judaism requires a deep commitment. Not only does one enter into a new community with its own customs and social rules, but a convert to Judaism must accept wholeheartedly God's sovereignty and undertake to fulfill all of the commandments of the Torah.

QUESTION: If a person sincerely wishes to convert to Judaism, will he or she be welcomed into the Jewish community?

ANSWER: The Torah demands numerous times that converts be loved and treated well. For example, it says in *Exodus* 12:49, "There shall be one law for the citizen and for the stranger [proselyte] who dwells among you," and in *Deuteronomy* 10:19, "You, too, must befriend the stranger [proselyte], for you were strangers in the land of Egypt."

QUESTION: Who were Onkelos and Aquila?

ANSWER: Onkelos and Aquila are two second-century Sages who are mentioned many times in the Talmud. Though they were both converts to Judaism (in fact, Aquila was a pagan priest), their accomplishments were extraordinary. Onkelos translated the Bible into Aramaic (the vernacular in Israel and Babylonia after the Babylonian exile), and his translation and commentary appear in almost every Hebrew Bible. Aquila was a disciple of Eli'ezer ben Hurkanos, Yehoshu'a ben Chananyah, and Rabbi Akiva—Akiva ben Yosef; he translated the Bible into Greek, although most of that translation was lost.[41]

QUESTION: Had Naomi rejected Ruth's desire to convert, what would Ruth have done?

ANSWER: Ruth's words, "Do not urge me to leave you...For wherever you go, I will go..." (1:16–17), brook no argument. The Sages explain that Ruth's decision was final: "Whether you accept me or not, I will convert. Please don't force me to turn to somebody else to instruct me about conversion."

QUESTION: The most oft-quoted sentence of the *Book of Ruth* is: [W]herever you go, I will go; wherever you lodge, I will lodge; your people shall be my people, and your God my God. Where you die, I will die, and there I will be buried" (1:16–17). What is the meaning of each of these declarations?

ANSWER: Before accepting Ruth as a convert, and in order to deter Ruth from making a rash decision, Naomi tested her. "Do you know that as a Jew you will be confined to your town on the Sabbath because it is forbidden to walk more than a short distance [about two thirds of a mile] outside the city limits on that day?" Undeterred, Ruth answered: "Wherever you go, I will go.

Naomi asked: "Do you know that your sleeping arrangements will be restricted, for a woman may not seclude herself with any man other than her husband?" Ruth replied simply: "Wherever you lodge, I will lodge."

"Do you realize," said Naomi, "that our nation differs from every other nation in 613 ways—the 613 commandments of the Torah?" "Your people are my people," responded Ruth.

"But are you fully aware that no form of idolatry is tolerated?" Naomi asked. "Your God is my God," said Ruth.

"These rules are not to be taken lightly," warned Naomi, "for some of them when violated are punishable by death." "I understand perfectly," answered Ruth. "Where you die, I will die. Indeed, if I violate the Torah and am sentenced to death, there I will be buried, with the criminals, apart from the rest of the nation."[42]

———

QUESTION: Verse 17 continues, "...Thus and more may the Lord do to me if anything but death parts me from you." What does this mean?

ANSWER: Ruth is making a serious commitment, one that will endure for the rest of her life. The only thing that can separate Ruth from Naomi is death. The Sages add that it was Ruth's hope that by converting she might also enjoy the afterlife with Naomi.

———

QUESTION: Does each person receive the same reward in the afterlife?

ANSWER: No two people face exactly the same challenges in life. Thus, one person's reward—or punishment!—is never identical with another's; each is based on the way he or she has conducted life on earth. Nonetheless, Ruth prayed to be reunited with Naomi in the afterlife.

———

QUESTION: How does Rashi interpret verses 16 and 17?

ANSWER: According to Rashi, Ruth told Naomi, "I will not leave you but follow you wherever you go, fully adhering to the Torah way of life. Were I to abandon you—if anything but death separated us—I know that God would increase the level of hardship I have already endured."

———

QUESTION: What happened then?

ANSWER: Naomi, convinced that Ruth was absolutely unshakable in her resolve to convert, "ceased to argue with her" (1:18).

——

QUESTION: What does this mean?

ANSWER: No longer did Naomi try to persuade Ruth to abandon her plan to convert. Moreover, now that Naomi was convinced of Ruth's sincerity, she didn't want to say anything that would jeopardize Ruth's resolve. So Naomi limited what she said.

——

QUESTION: What did Naomi not say to Ruth?

ANSWER: Naomi avoided a discussion of Torah law.

——

QUESTION: Why did Naomi do this?

ANSWER: Conversion is a difficult process. A child who is born into a Jewish family slowly learns the mitzvot of the Torah. A person considering converting to Judaism may feel intimidated or overwhelmed by the numerous commandments and strictures. Once we are convinced of a person's sincerity to convert, we try to work slowly with that individual so that he or she does not have a change of heart.

——

QUESTION: What was so extraordinary about Ruth's conversion?

ANSWER: Let us remember that Ruth was of royal descent, the daughter of the king of Moab. The fact that she was willing to leave behind everything she had known to convert to Judaism earns her our utmost respect. According to many of our Sages, Ruth was the first well-known *individual* to convert to Judaism. The qualities she demonstrated—perseverance, thirst for knowledge, and sincere devotion—established the foundation for future practice.

———

QUESTION: What is the conversion process according to Jewish Law?

ANSWER: First and foremost, a convert must accept the Jewish belief in one God and all the laws of the Torah as personally binding. After he or she has engaged in intense study with a rabbi or qualified teacher, the convert comes before a *beit din*, a rabbinical court consisting of three rabbis who question the convert about Jewish laws and rituals and before whom the convert vows to perform all the mitzvot. The convert then immerses him- or herself in a mikvah ("ritual bath") and recites a special blessing. Following immersion, the members of the *beit din* will declare the individual a Jew. If the convert is male, he must have been circumcised prior to coming before the *beit din*. If he had been previously circumcised, a ceremonial drop of blood is drawn. At the time of the Temple, a convert would bring a special sacrifice; obviously, since the destruction of the First and Second Temples, sacrifices are no longer performed.[43]

QUESTION: Did Naomi's acceptance of Ruth's sincere desire to convert mark a change in their relationship?

ANSWER: Definitely! Whereas earlier verses referred to Naomi and her daughters-in-law (verse 6, for example, begins, "She [Naomi] started out with her daughters-in-law to return from the country of Moab... "), the text now reads that "the two [Naomi and Ruth] went on until they reached Bethlehem" (1:19). Once Ruth converted, she was on equal footing with Naomi. Naomi saw herself and Ruth not as mother-in-law and daughter-in-law but as two friends who were traveling together. Ruth, however, continued to defer to Naomi out of the great respect she had for her and because Naomi was her elder.

QUESTION: Where do we find similar language in the Torah?

ANSWER: When God commanded Abraham to go and sacrifice his son Isaac, the text says that Abraham and Isaac "went together" (*Genesis* 22:6)—father and son had their hearts set on fulfilling God's difficult challenge. In the *Book of Ruth*, the two women, Naomi and Ruth, knew that the journey upon which they had embarked also would be difficult, yet their hearts were set on moving ahead, no matter what awaited them.

———

QUESTION: How long did it take Naomi and Ruth to travel on foot from Moab to Bethlehem?

ANSWER: The Sages tell us that it was but a few days' journey.

———

QUESTION: Naomi and Ruth traveled alone, without male escort. Wasn't that dangerous? Did anything happen along the way?

ANSWER: There is no record of any untoward incidents on their way to Bethlehem. It is quite possible that they received divine protection. It was Orpah, who the Midrash says, abandoned Ruth and Naomi and was attacked on her way home.

———

QUESTION: When Ruth and Naomi arrived in Bethlehem, we are told the city "buzzed with excitement over them" (1:19). Why?

ANSWER: According to the Sages, Boaz's wife died on the very day of Ruth and Naomi's arrival.[44] Between the funeral that was taking place and the surprise of Naomi's return, the city was abuzz.

———

QUESTION: What was the significance of these two events?

ANSWER: Boaz was a leader of his generation. The whole town must have accompanied him to bury his beloved wife. Imagine the townspeople's surprise upon returning from the burial to see Naomi and Ruth. Their leader's wife had just been laid to rest when who appears but Naomi, the wife of their past leader, Elimelech. How dramatic!

——

QUESTION: It is said that God prepares the cure before he produces the illness. How does this apply to our story?

ANSWER: The Sages teach that Ruth was destined to marry Boaz. Though she was not yet ready to do so, it would happen in the near future. God set the stage for this great event: as soon as Boaz's wife died, Ruth arrived in Bethlehem.

——

QUESTION: Why else were the people of Bethlehem in such an uproar over Naomi's return?

ANSWER: Naomi's husband, Elimelech, had been both influential and extremely wealthy. As the wife of such an important man, Naomi was remembered as a well-dressed woman who never traveled alone but was always escorted by maids and servants. Naomi was said, according to the Midrash, to have owned so much jewelry that whenever the girls of Bethlehem needed to adorn themselves, they borrowed finery from her.[45] What a contrast the returning Naomi was, barefoot, her tattered clothes gray with dust, her face sunken from hunger.

———

QUESTION: Did the townspeople immediately recognize Naomi?

ANSWER: The people of Bethlehem already thought it strange to see two women traveling without escort. Imagine their astonishment when the women got closer and the townspeople saw their haggard appearance. When the residents of Bethlehem finally recognized Naomi, their shock was complete.

———

QUESTION: If the city of Bethlehem was astir "over them," meaning Naomi and Ruth, why did the townswomen say only "Can this be Naomi?" (1:19) and not speak of Ruth?

ANSWER: Ruth was a strange presence, but the townspeople could not get over the utter contrast between the Naomi who left Israel and the Naomi who returned. Many found it hard to believe she was the same person. On a deeper level, the Talmud explains, the devout people of Bethlehem were being taught an important lesson: see what happens to somebody who leaves the land of Israel![46] Naomi left Bethlehem to avoid a famine; she returned a starving woman, a stark punishment to be sure.

———

QUESTION: When the women of Bethlehem recognized Naomi, she said to them, "Do not call me Naomi...Call me Mara, for [God] has made my life bitter" (1:20). Why?

ANSWER: The name Naomi means "pleasant," and it described Naomi in her previous life in Bethlehem, both in appearance and in her manner toward others. Naomi, which so suited her before, was ironic now, for there was nothing pleasant about the circumstances in which she found herself. Mara means "embittered one": "I went away full, and the Lord has brought me back empty....[T]he Lord has dealt harshly with me...." (1:20–21). What a bitter blow these changes were for her to bear!

———

QUESTION: Was Naomi really a bitter person?

ANSWER: Probably not. The *Book of Ruth* portrays Naomi as a virtuous woman who accepted the decree of God, whether for good or for evil: as the expression goes, *gam zo le-tovah*—"it's all for the best." Though her situation was a bitter one, Naomi herself was not necessarily bitter.

———

QUESTION: Why change her name?

ANSWER: Sometimes people with good fortune suffer terrible reversals. To understand the painful positions in which they find themselves, we must remember their former names—how they used to be. By asking to be called Mara, Naomi acknowledged God's judgment, saying: "I'm totally impoverished, I have nothing; there is no need to be reminded of my former fame and wealth to grasp my actual bitterness and heartache."

———

QUESTION: Why did Naomi return to Bethlehem instead of going to another town, perhaps a place where nobody knew her?

ANSWER: Bethlehem was the capital of Jewish life in those days. It was situated close to the border with Moab and was Naomi's hometown, the place where her sons had been born, a place with great sentimental attachment. As we will learn later on in the *Book of Ruth*, Naomi had relatives in Bethlehem and business to attend to as well, namely the disposition of her husband's property.

———

QUESTION: Verse 22 indicates that Ruth also returned to the land of Israel from the fields of Moab. Isn't this rather puzzling since Ruth had never before set foot in the land of Israel?

ANSWER: Ruth was a descendent of Lot, nephew of the patriarch Abraham. Lot survived the destruction of the cities of Sodom and Gomorrah with his two daughters, who later bore him two sons, Amon and Moab, fathers of the Ammonite and Moabite nations. The very reason for Lot's rescue, the Sages say, was to bring into the world two righteous converts: Ruth the Moabite, from whom King David would descend, and Naamah, a righteous Ammonite, wife of King Solomon, whose son, Rehoboam, would succeed his father as the king of Israel (*1Kings* 14:21). The word *return* that appears in verse 22 comes from the Hebrew root *shuv,* which also can mean "repent" or "return to the Jewish faith." With Ruth's lineage in mind, we can understand her conversion as a return to the Jewish faith of her ancestors and a penitence for the evil deeds of her Moabite predecessors. By repairing their evil through her conversion to Judaism, according to the Jewish mystical tradition, Ruth was engaged in *tikkun olam,* "repairing the world."

———

QUESTION: The last sentence of chapter 1 tells us that Ruth and Naomi arrived in Bethlehem "at the beginning of the barley harvest" (1:22). When did the barley harvest take place?

ANSWER: The barley harvest began on the second night of Passover and was marked by the bringing of the *omer*—a sheaf of newly harvested barley—to the priest (*Leviticus* 23:9–14; in the days of the Temple, the offering would, of course, have been brought there). The barley was roasted, ground into fine flour, mixed with oil, and then offered in sacrifice. Following the *omer* festivities, the Israelites proceeded with the barley harvest and were permitted to eat from the new crop. Though we do not know the exact date on which Naomi and Ruth arrived in Bethlehem, it is quite possible that they arrived on Passover or shortly thereafter.

Chapter 2

Synopsis

Having returned to Bethlehem with nothing but the clothes on their backs, Ruth set out to the barley fields to gather grain for herself and Naomi. Providentially, she chose to glean in the field of Boaz, a relative of Naomi (although Ruth will not learn this fact until the end of chapter 2), a man considered the leader of his generation and held in high esteem by all. Impressed by Ruth's many qualities—her care and concern for Naomi, the fact that she had relinquished her land and her faith to embrace Judaism—Boaz treats her with great respect and compassion, arranging for her to glean exclusively in his fields until the end of the harvest season.

———

QUESTION: What does the name Boaz mean?

ANSWER: The word *az* (*oz*) in Hebrew means "strength" or "vigor." Boaz's name means "there is strength in him."

———

QUESTION: What do we learn about Boaz at the beginning of chapter 2?

ANSWER: We learn first, in fact, that Boaz was an *ish gibor chayil* (2:1), a Hebrew expression meaning "a man of substance" or "a man of valor" (*gibor* means "strength"; *chayil*, "valor"), and second that he was related to Naomi through her late husband, Elimelech.

——

QUESTION: As we discussed in the previous chapter, the word *ish* indicates an important person. In chapter 1, verse 1, Elimelech is referred to as an *ish* of Bethlehem; in chapter 2, verse 1, Boaz is referred to as an *ish* of valor. How do Boaz and Elimelech compare?

ANSWER: Both Elimelech and Boaz were men of stature, community leaders. But the comparison ends there. Elimelech failed the test given to him by God, and, like a captain who jumps ship in the midst of a raging storm, leaving passengers and crew to fend for themselves, Elimelech abandoned his fellow Israelites during their time of need, the famine. On the other hand, Boaz was not simply a person of stature but a man of valor.[1] Some time after Elimelech left Bethlehem, Boaz assumed leadership of the town and its inhabitants. As the *Book of Ruth* unfolds, Boaz's inner strength, perceptive nature, and warm personality are revealed.

——

QUESTION: Does the phrase *ish gibor chayil* indicate that Boaz was physically strong?

ANSWER: It is possible that Boaz was a strong man. However, according to our Sages, Boaz was eighty years old when he met Ruth, an age when someone is unlikely to be characterized by his physical prowess.[2]

———

QUESTION: What then is the meaning of *ish gibor chayil*?

ANSWER: The term implies inner strength.[3]

———

QUESTION: What does it say in the Scriptures about strength?

ANSWER: In *Proverbs* 16:32, King Solomon writes: "...One who masters his evil spirit is greater than one who conquers a city."[4]

———

QUESTION: What does the Mishnah say about strength?

ANSWER: The Mishnah quotes Shimon Ben Zoma, who, in *Ethics of the Fathers*, asks, "Who is strong? One who is capable of controlling his evil instincts." In other words, when one takes measure of another human being, inner strength is more important than physical might.

———

QUESTION: How were Elimelech and Boaz related?

ANSWER: Salmon, father of Boaz, was Elimelech's brother, making Boaz the nephew of Elimelech (see chart).

———

QUESTION: Were Boaz and Naomi related?

ANSWER: Naomi's father also was a brother of Salmon.[5] Thus, Naomi was Boaz's first cousin and Elimelech's niece.

———

QUESTION: Why did the townspeople of Bethlehem seemingly ignore Naomi and Ruth when they returned from Moab?

ANSWER: There are several explanations. First, the people of Bethlehem remembered with anger how Elimelech and Naomi left Bethlehem, taking all their possessions with them and leaving nothing behind for the poor and starving. Second, Naomi returned with a Moabite woman; the townspeople were reluctant to socialize with Naomi for this reason. Third, Boaz's wife had just died, and the townspeople were focused on Boaz's loss.[6]

———

QUESTION: Why didn't Naomi immediately contact Boaz upon her return to Bethlehem?

ANSWER: As we discussed, Boaz's wife had died on the very day that Naomi and Ruth reached Bethlehem.[7] It would have been improper of Naomi to have approached Boaz with her problems at the time of his wife's death. Additionally, Naomi may have been unsure of Boaz's attitude toward her for having left Israel during the time of famine and for having returned to Bethlehem with a Moabite daughter-in-law. Naomi also was a proud woman, unused to asking for charity.[8]

———

QUESTION: Rather than burden Boaz with her problems, why didn't Naomi simply pay a *shivah* call (a visit to the home of mourners) to express her sorrow at Boaz's wife's passing?

ANSWER: According to the Sages,[9] Naomi was afraid that her presence would be unwelcome in the house of mourning and that it would only add to Boaz's pain.

———

QUESTION: What did Ruth propose to her mother-in law regarding providing for their survival?

ANSWER: Ruth understood that the burden of providing for her own and Naomi's needs rested entirely on her shoulders. Though she was of royal descent, she humbly asked Naomi's permission to glean grain dropped in the field (called *leket* in Hebrew; see below) by the barley harvesters.[10]

——

QUESTION: Why does the text refer to "Ruth the Moabite" (2:2) instead of just "Ruth"?

ANSWER: Although Naomi and Boaz were related, Naomi demonstrated strength of character in not burdening Boaz with her problems. Ruth also demonstrated great strength of character. She assumed responsibility for providing for herself and her mother-in-law, willingly gleaning in the fields for grain like other poor people did.[11]

——

QUESTION: Women, as well as men, were hired to work in the fields during harvest time. Why didn't Ruth want to be hired as a worker rather than accept charity?

ANSWER: Some commentators say that Ruth would have preferred to have been hired as a paid field hand. Naomi, however, wanted to make clear to Boaz exactly how serious her and Ruth's situation was. By sending Ruth to glean with the other poor, Naomi hoped to elicit Boaz's sympathy and that Boaz would reestablish contact with her.[12]

——

QUESTION: Who taught Ruth that the poor were permitted to collect crops in the field?

ANSWER: Many Sages say that Naomi taught Ruth these laws, specifically the laws of *leket*.[13]

QUESTION: When did Naomi teach Ruth about the laws of *leket*?

ANSWER: According to the Sages, Naomi taught Ruth about the harvesting laws while they walked from Moab to Bethlehem.[14]

QUESTION: Why didn't Ruth ask Naomi to accompany her to collect grain in the fields?

ANSWER: Naomi had been a prominent, wealthy resident of Bethlehem before leaving for Moab. Ruth understood that Naomi might feel ashamed having to accept charity upon her return and sought to shield her mother-in-law from potential humiliation. Ruth, therefore, put aside her own pride and took the entire job of providing for the two of them upon herself.[15]

QUESTION: What rights did the poor have in the fields of wealthy landowners?

ANSWER: The Torah (*Leviticus* 19:9–10, 23:22;

Deuteronomy 14:22–29, 24:19–21, 26:12–14) specifies three types of tithes benefiting the poor that are given from the harvest. They are called *leket*, *shikhchah*, and *pe'ah*.

QUESTION: What is *leket*?

ANSWER: *Leket*, which means "gleaning," refers to stalks dropped by the harvesters in the field. The harvesters are not permitted to go back and pick them up. Instead, the poor are permitted to follow behind the harvesters and gather up anything that has been dropped. This is what Ruth did.[16]

QUESTION: Is *leket* restricted to particular kinds of produce?

ANSWER: Yes. Unlike *pe'ah* (see below), *leket* is restricted to grain fields, orchards, and vineyards.[17]

QUESTION: What is *shikhchah*?

ANSWER: *Shikhchah*, which means "something forgotten," refers to sheaves forgotten in the field by the harvesters, or, in the case of orchards, to one or two trees that may have been left unpicked. The harvesters are forbidden to go back and pick up the sheaves or pick the missed fruit. They must leave them for the poor.

QUESTION: What is *pe'ah*?

ANSWER: The word *pe'ah* means "corner" and refers to corners of the fields that should not be harvested but left for the poor.

———

QUESTION: How much grain can be gleaned from a corner of a field?

ANSWER: The owner of a field must leave at least one-sixtieth of the harvest for the poor. If the crop is especially good or there are many poor people, the farmer should leave more.[18]

———

QUESTION: Does *pe'ah* apply only to fields of grain?

ANSWER: Not at all. Whether a farmer grows fruit trees or vegetables, he must leave a section of the orchard or field untouched for the poor. This applies to all food.

———

QUESTION: Who is entitled to *leket, shikhchah, and pe'ah*?

ANSWER: The Sages considered a person who had less then fourteen meals per week in need of charitable support, and the community was obligated to assist that individual and his or her family.[19] Moses Maimonides, the twelfth-century Jewish philosopher known as the Rambam, agreed, defining a poor person as one who did not have enough money or food for two meals a day.[20]

QUESTION: During the Middle Ages, when Jews no longer lived in a predominantly agricultural society, new forms of charity replaced *leket, shikhchah,* and *pe'ah.* What were some of them?

ANSWER: Two of these new forms of charity were *tamchu'i,* a daily distribution of food, much like a soup kitchen today, and *kuppah,* a charity box (also called a *tzedakah* box, or *pushka*), from which funds were distributed to the needy. Giving charity, in Hebrew *tzedakah,* has been a hallmark of Jewish practice throughout history.[21]

QUESTION: If one has a great deal of money but no access to it, is he or she entitled to receive charitable tithes?

ANSWER: Yes. If, for example, a person is traveling and forgets to bring money along, the Torah considers him temporarily poor, and he is permitted to receive all the benefits allotted to the poor.[22]

QUESTION: What did the poor do with the grain, fruit, and vegetables they gathered?

ANSWER: They were free to do whatever they wished with the harvest because it was considered their property. They could eat it or sell it.

———

QUESTION: Did these laws apply only in Israel?

ANSWER: The laws of tithing applied only in Israel. However, the obligation to aid the poor has been assumed by Jews the world over.[23]

———

QUESTION: Do the laws of tithing apply today?

ANSWER: Not only did the laws of tithing apply only in Israel, but they applied only until the destruction of the Second Temple. These laws could not be fulfilled once the Temple was destroyed. However, the mandate to give charity remains strong, and the *Shulchan Arukh*, the Code of Jewish Law, requires Jews to tithe—give a tenth of their earnings to *tzedakah*.

———

QUESTION: What is the purpose of tithes for the poor?

ANSWER: The commandments of *leket*, *shikhchah*, and *pe'ah* serve a twofold purpose. The first, obviously, is to provide the hungry with food. The second is to teach those whom God has endowed with plenitude to share their wealth with others.[24] We must not be selfish and hoard our bounty but learn to be philanthropic. Additionally, we recognize that God is the owner of everything in the world and the source of all blessing and success. As part of our obligation to our Creator, God Almighty, we are obligated to share a portion of our God-endowed prosperity with all the needy inhabitants of the globe.

QUESTION: If the poor had the right to glean in the fields, why did Ruth say: "...I would like to go to the fields and glean among the ears of grain, behind someone who may show me kindness" (2:2)? Wasn't Ruth entitled to the *leket*, whether or not she found favor in the landowner's eyes and he showed her kindness?

ANSWER: She certainly was. Nobody fit the definition of "poor" better than Ruth. She was a convert to Judaism, with no blood relatives to support her emotionally or financially. Of course she had her mother-in-law, Naomi, but although Naomi was a marvelous teacher and example—a very special mentor, indeed—Naomi was herself without resources and felt bereft.

QUESTION: Why then did Ruth want to glean "behind someone who may show me kindness"?

ANSWER: Ruth was a singularly modest woman; despite her poverty, she was descended from royalty and demonstrated exceptional conduct. Although she was entitled to receive grain for the poor, she would not take it if the owner of the field did not agree to her doing so.[25]

___

QUESTION: We learn later in the story that Naomi owned land. Why did Ruth have to gather stalks in a field belonging to somebody else?

ANSWER: Naomi's land had been vacant for over ten years. No crops had been planted, and the fields would yield no harvest.

___

QUESTION: As a landowner, would Naomi have been permitted to eat the *leket* gathered by Ruth?

ANSWER: Yes. Naomi may have owned fields, but they hadn't been worked in many years, and nobody would have bought her land at the beginning of the harvest season; Naomi would have had to wait until the harvest period was over before she could hope to sell the fields to one of Elimelech's family members. The only way for Naomi to eat was to share the *leket* gleaned by Ruth.

___

QUESTION: When Ruth told Naomi that she planned to glean in the fields, Naomi replied: "*Lechi biti*" (2:2). What does this mean?

ANSWER: The words mean "Go my daughter." Naomi acknowledged Ruth's many sacrifices. Although Ruth was not Naomi's real daughter and although she wasn't born Jewish, Ruth behaved as a true daughter of Israel.[26]

——

QUESTION: What are the recurrent themes in chapter 2, indeed in the entire *Book of Ruth*?

ANSWER: Humility, kindness, and modesty, all of which contribute to *tikkun olam*, making the world a better place. Time and again the text stresses these praiseworthy traits seen in Ruth.

——

QUESTION: How important is humility in Judaism?

ANSWER: According to the prophet Micah, God requires three things of man: "To do justly, to love mercy, and to walk humbly with God" (*Micah* 6:8). Two of the greatest figures in Judaism, Abraham and Moses, embodied humility in their love for their fellow man and their sensitivity to the feelings and needs of others. Judaism teaches that man is not alone in the world but under God's constant gaze. Man's conduct and behavior must always reflect this.

——

QUESTION: What is humility?

ANSWER: More than a character trait, humility is a way of life. It is reflected not only in our behavior but in our thoughts. If we believe that God is always watching us and that we are accountable to God for our every action, we will conduct ourselves properly and treat others appropriately.

———

QUESTION: Why is Ruth's humility especially striking?

ANSWER: Children of royal descent usually are raised to believe that they are better than common folk. When such a person shows great humility, it is the sign of an outstanding personality.

———

QUESTION: Verse 3 begins: "and off [Ruth] went. She came and gleaned in a field, behind the reapers . . ." Why does it say both "went" and "came"?

ANSWER: The simple explanation is that Ruth left the security of the dwelling she shared with Naomi to explore unfamiliar territory. Despite the uncertainties, Ruth did not hesitate to go to the fields to provide food for Naomi. Another interpretation is that the use of the words *going* ("went") and *coming* ("came") indicate that every day during the three months of the harvest season Ruth went out to the fields in the morning, spent the whole day gleaning, and then came home every evening.[27]

———

QUESTION: Is there another interpretation?

ANSWER: The Sages say that Ruth came and went until she found a suitable field in which to glean. If she heard the harvesters using coarse language, she would try a different field—yet another indication of her modesty—until she happened upon Boaz's land.[28] The Midrash explains the verse to mean that Ruth went and marked her way. In other words: Ruth would not walk to a field without carefully marking the way home, insuring that she would not get lost on the way back and find herself in an unpleasant or dangerous situation in which she might be harassed by some of the coarser field hands.[29]

———

QUESTION: Verse 3 continues: "and, as luck would have it, it was the piece of land belonging to Boaz . . ." Was it accidental that Ruth found herself in Boaz's field?

ANSWER: From Ruth's perspective, it was completely accidental that she wound up in one of Boaz's fields. Ruth considered herself lucky to have found a safe place in which to gather the *leket*. Boaz was an exceptionally righteous man whose pleasant ways clearly influenced the behavior of his workers. But, in fact, Ruth's steps were divinely guided. Indeed, the phrase *vayiker mikreha*—"as luck would have it"—can be understood as "this was made to happen." One midrash says that a divine emissary (angel) led Ruth to Boaz's field.[30]

———

QUESTION: Is this phenomenon unusual?

ANSWER: Not really. The Sages say that all of man's actions are guided by the Divine Presence.[31]

———

QUESTION: If all of our actions are divinely directed, does this mean that there is no free will?

ANSWER: Certainly not. Judaism teaches that man chooses whether to do good or to do evil, but that his destiny is guided by God. For example, it is recorded in *Genesis* that God appeared to Abraham and told him that his descendents would one day be enslaved (in Egypt; *Genesis* 15:13–14), but also that Abraham's descendents would number the stars in the sky and inherit the Land of Israel. These prophecies reveal predestination. On the other hand, it is written in the Bible (*Deuteronomy* 30:19), "...I have put before you life and death, blessing and curse. Choose life—if you and your offspring would live—by loving the Lord your God, heeding His commandments, and holding fast to Him." This demonstrates the concept of freedom of choice.

The Jewish tradition firmly maintains that there are ways of altering one's destiny. For example, on Rosh Hashanah—the Jewish New Year—the fate of every creature is decided, and the names of those who will live in the coming year are inscribed in the Book of Life. However, Judaism teaches that repentance, prayer, and charity can reverse God's unfavorable judgment.

Jewish philosophers and Jewish mystics through the ages have had some very different views about Divine Providence, God's hand in the world. Maimonides, for example, believed that God watches over the world from above, making sure that the sun rises and sets each day, but that He does not interfere in a person's actions or decisions. This school of thought is called *hashgachah kelalit* (*hashgachah* means "Providence," *kelalit* means "comprehensive"). The Kabbalists, the Chasidim, and twentieth-century Jewish philosophers such as Rabbi Joseph Soloveichik and Rabbi Abraham Joshua Heschel, on the other hand, subscribed to *hashgachah peratit* (*peratit* means "individual"). According to this school of thought, man and God are in constant dialogue; God is involved in each of our lives every minute of every day, wherever we are.[32]

QUESTION: Did God shape the destiny of Ruth and Boaz?

ANSWER: Ruth and Boaz married. King David was descended from them, and the Messiah will one day descend from him. While Ruth and Boaz made their own decisions, God guided their destiny; these were not simple events: the future of the Jewish people was at stake. Outwardly, Ruth and Boaz seemed to have little in common; if God had not brought them together, they might not have found each other.

QUESTION: Why does verse 3 say that Ruth gleaned *behind* the reapers?

ANSWER: According to one commentary, Ruth was an attractive woman whose beauty would catch the attention of any man. Out of extreme modesty, Ruth walked behind the harvesters so as not to draw attention to herself. Yet her unusual beauty did not pass unnoticed.[33]

———

QUESTION: Why does verse 4 open with the words, "Presently Boaz arrived from Bethlehem"? Aren't Ruth, Naomi, and Boaz in Bethlehem already?

ANSWER: Boaz's fields were likely outside of town; he left Bethlehem proper to go to his fields and inspect the work that was going on in them. The word *ve-hineh*, "presently" or "behold," may indicate an unusual occurrence—Boaz normally would not have come to the fields, but God led him there on that day to meet Ruth.[34]

———

QUESTION: How did Boaz greet his workers when he reached the field?

ANSWER: Boaz said, "The Lord be with you!" (2:4).

———

QUESTION: What do we learn from the way Boaz greeted his workers?

ANSWER: We learn that an employer must not speak to his or her employees in a condescending manner. On the contrary, one must use the name of God when wishing peace and blessing on others.

———

QUESTION: The harvesters responded "The Lord bless you!" to Boaz's greeting. What does this indicate?

ANSWER: It shows that Boaz's employees felt honored by Boaz's greeting and graciously replied in a like manner.

———

QUESTION: Is it proper to mention God's name when greeting a friend?

ANSWER: We recognize God's omnipresence and omnipotence in every task we undertake, no matter how mundane. Following Boaz's example, it is customary to mention God's name whenever one greets a friend. Every person is created in the image of God. By mentioning God's name when we greet a friend, we acknowledge our friend's divine spark.[35]

———

QUESTION: What was so special about the greeting that Boaz and his harvesters exchanged?

ANSWER: Any heartfelt greeting is more than the acknowledgment of another's presence; it is the acknowledgement of the blessing of *being* in another's presence.

———

QUESTION: How do we greet one another today?

ANSWER: It is customary to greet a friend by saying "Shalom"—"peace." We ask God to grant our friends—and all of mankind—peace. Indeed, Shalom is one of God's many names, which characterize Him by His attributes.[36]

———

QUESTION: What important element of the Jewish laws of mourning do we learn from Boaz's behavior?

ANSWER: During the seven-day period of mourning known as *shivah*, the social niceties of greeting are suspended, and it is unseemly for the visitor to greet the mourner. Instead, the mourner initiates conversation with the visitor. Boaz, who had been in mourning for his wife, signaled that the *shivah* period was over when he arrived at his field and extended greetings to his field hands. His blessing, "The Lord be with you!" indicates that he accepted his loss as God's will and was not bitter.[37]

———

QUESTION: Why did Boaz ask his manager in verse 5, "Whose girl is that?"

ANSWER: Boaz inquired about the poor woman gleaning behind the harvesters because Ruth had caught his attention.

QUESTION: Boaz had just returned to his farm after an absence of a week or more. Isn't it strange that he would ask his manager about a person gleaning in his fields rather than about the state of his business affairs?

ANSWER: Ruth was so strikingly different from all the other gleaners that Boaz felt compelled to inquire about her.[38]

QUESTION: What set Ruth apart from the other gleaners?

ANSWER: Some poor women tried to curry favor with the harvesters in hopes of receiving extra food. Others picked from places in which they did not have permission to glean. Ruth, however, was a scrupulously modest gleaner, never socializing with Boaz's employees lest they give her more than she was entitled to, and never gleaning from areas of the field that were not open to the poor. Ruth's exceptional behavior caught Boaz's attention.

QUESTION: How did the manager reply to Boaz's question about Ruth?

ANSWER: The manager's answer was rather puzzling. Instead of identifying Ruth by name, he referred to her as the Moabite girl who had returned with Naomi from Moab, not even mentioning that she was Naomi's daughter-in-law. The manager continued with a description of Ruth's request for permission to glean behind the harvesters and added that she had been on her feet from early in the morning.

The manager's response to Boaz can be interpreted in two different ways, in a negative light—deprecatingly—or in a positive light—complimentary to Ruth.

———

QUESTION: Why did the manager refer to Ruth as both a Moabite *na'arah*—a Moabite "girl"—and the one "who came back with Naomi from the country of Moab" (2:6)?

ANSWER: The manager may have tried deliberately, yet subtly, to diminish Ruth in Boaz's eyes by referring to her as a Moabite "girl," thinking that Boaz was attracted to Ruth for her good looks, or that he was too prominent a figure or too old for Ruth. By emphasizing her Moabite origins twice, the manager also may have been implying that Ruth's conversion was not valid.

Boaz clearly sensed Ruth's aura of humility. The manager tried to denigrate this as well: "True, she excels in modesty, but not because it is one of her inner qualities, simply because she is good at copying Naomi and following Naomi's directives." In other words, Ruth was no more than a well-trained student who understood the lesson of her master but had not internalized the teaching.

———

QUESTION: The manager continued in verse 7: "[Ruth] said, 'Please let me glean and gather among the sheaves behind the reapers.' She has been on her feet ever since she came this morning..." What was he trying to convey to Boaz with this information?

ANSWER: The poor were permitted to gather only stalks, not sheaves of grain. The manager may have been trying to imply that Ruth was stealing sheaves of grain rather than collecting the stalks to which she was entitled. However, Ruth told Naomi very clearly in verse 2 that she planned to gather stalks (*shibalim*) rather than sheaves (*amarim*).

———

QUESTION: As we mentioned above, the manager's statement, Ruth is the one "who came back with Naomi from the country of Moab," can be understood in a positive light. How so?

ANSWER: Perhaps the manager thought that Boaz wanted to know why a Moabite was gleaning in his field. "She is not a Moabite, but a young woman of exemplary character who converted to Judaism and returned to Bethlehem with Naomi and who is now caring for Naomi." By stressing that Ruth was a young woman, the manager indicated that Ruth was of childbearing age. As even greater proof of Ruth's virtue, the manager recounted how Ruth asked for permission—though no permission was needed—to glean in Boaz's field.

QUESTION: The reference in verse 7 to the hut in which Ruth was said to have rested is puzzling. Was it common to have a small hut in which workers could rest from the sun or have a drink of water?

ANSWER: Yes. However, some commentators believe the hut refers to Naomi and Ruth's home and that Ruth went home for a short period to rest.[39]

QUESTION: How did Boaz react to his manager's answer?

ANSWER: Boaz didn't reply. If he sensed his manager's hostility, he knew that it would be futile to argue with a fool. Nothing Boaz could say would convince his manager to change his unfavorable opinion of Ruth, if that's what it was.

QUESTION: The first words Boaz spoke to Ruth were: "Listen to me, daughter" (2:8). Why did Boaz refer to Ruth as *biti*, "[my] daughter"?

ANSWER: Boaz recognized Ruth as a true daughter of Israel (in the same way that Naomi did when she referred to Ruth as *biti* in verse 2). He could see that she was familiar with Jewish law—she knew the rules of gleaning—and whereas many of the female harvesters socialized and flirted with the male harvesters, Ruth was not garrulous or talkative. She impressed Boaz with her dignified behavior and humility. Boaz spoke to Ruth in a respectful way to make sure that she would feel comfortable.

Boaz's choice of language may have indicated public acceptance of Ruth's conversion, and by referring to her as *biti*, he also may have recognized their familial relationship.

———

QUESTION: Boaz urged Ruth to continue gleaning in his field with the words, "... Don't go to glean in another field. Don't go elsewhere, but stay here close to my girls" (2:8). Why did Boaz say both *al telkhi lilkot be-sadeh acher* (" Don't go to glean in another field") and *ve-gam lo ta'avuri mi-zeh* ("Don't go elsewhere")?

ANSWER: Boaz exhorted Ruth to remain not only on his property but in the very field in which she was gleaning. Not only was Ruth assured of permission to stay in the company of Boaz's female employees for the entire harvest season, but she also was spared the embarrassment of having to beg for food from different landowners.

A poor person would leave a field for two reasons, one, because the crop was depleted; two, because the owner of the field was inhospitable. Boaz twice urged Ruth to remain where she was because neither reason applied.[40]

———

QUESTION: In what way did Boaz demonstrate his obedience to God?

ANSWER: Boaz knew that his fortune was the result of God's blessing. If poor people were not welcome in his field, he would not be worthy of God's benevolence. Ruth represented not only the poor, but the widow and the convert. All are in need of aid, and all are a source of blessing to those who aid them (*Deuteronomy* 15:10).[41]

———

QUESTION: Boaz said to Ruth, "Keep your eyes on the field" (2:9). What is the meaning of this phrase?

ANSWER: As a righteous woman, Ruth surely possessed a "good eye" as opposed to an "evil eye." Boaz was saying to Ruth, "Don't think that I am doing you a favor. Your good eye—your presence in my field—brings me blessing." Often, the rich think that they are doing the poor a favor by giving charity. In fact, it is the other way around. The poor bring God's gratitude and blessing to the rich.[42]

———

QUESTION: Why else didn't Boaz want Ruth to glean in any other field?

ANSWER: Once he learned that Ruth was such an exceptional woman and the daughter-in-law of his cousin, Naomi, Boaz felt responsible for Ruth and wanted to keep an eye on her.[43]

According to the Targum, the Aramaic translation of and commentary on the Bible that came into use following the Babylonian exile, Boaz also didn't want Ruth to glean in any other field lest she renounce Judaism, her new religion.

———

QUESTION: At the end of verse 8, Boaz instructed Ruth to "stay here close to my girls." In verse 9, he continued to give Ruth very explicit instructions about gleaning in his field: "Keep your eyes on the field [my girls] are reaping, and follow them. I have ordered the men not to molest you. And when you are thirsty, go to the jars and drink some of [the water] that the men have drawn." Why does he tell her all this?

ANSWER: Boaz wanted her to socialize with his female workers. His manager had expressed concern, albeit obliquely, about a possible relationship between Boaz and Ruth. To avoid any unwanted talk, Boaz preferred that Ruth stick close to the other women in the field and not spend time alone with him. Though Boaz had instructed his male employees to leave Ruth alone, he wanted Ruth to work behind his female employees as an added buffer. On top of that, Boaz invited Ruth to help herself to a drink if she got thirsty.[44]

—

QUESTION: Boaz said to Ruth, "I have ordered the men not to molest you." Why is the term "molest" used?

ANSWER: Boaz believed that every human being should be treated fairly and with respect. He informed Ruth publicly—so that everybody could hear—that she was free to collect as much barley as she wanted. Boaz didn't want his male workers to take advantage of Ruth in any way because she had been born a Moabite and was a recent convert to Judaism.[45]

—

QUESTION: Why didn't Boaz instruct Ruth simply to draw her own water?

ANSWER: According to the Sages, there were three wells in Boaz's field. Ruth would have had to travel quite a distance to reach them. Boaz wanted to prevent Ruth from wasting her strength by drawing her own water and wasting her gleaning time by walking so far to the wells.[46]

The mention of wells also reminds us of the story of Eliezer, whom Abraham had sent to seek a wife for his son, Isaac, and Rebekah, who would become Isaac's bride. Eliezer asked God for a sign indicating that he had chosen well for Isaac: "Let the maiden to whom I say, 'Please, lower your jar so that I may drink,' and who answers, 'Drink, and I will also water your camels,' be the one you have decreed for Isaac" (*Genesis* 24:43–44). Just as Eliezer recognized that Rebekah was the bride selected by God for Isaac, so, perhaps, did Boaz divinely intuit that he and Ruth were destined to share a special relationship.

———

QUESTION: We discussed the fact that Elimelech failed God's test by deserting his fellow Israelites during a time of famine. Did God also test Boaz?

ANSWER: One of the tests of the rich is how they treat the poor. Are they respectful or condescending? Friendly or cold? Although Elimelech helped those less fortunate, he was a reluctant giver and not especially generous. It is said that he would rather throw good food away than give it to the poor.

Boaz, also a very wealthy man, a landowner and community leader, was similarly tested by God. He proved himself to be a kind, giving person, sensitive to the feelings of others, as demonstrated by the way in which he greeted his harvesters and in his first interaction with Ruth.

———

QUESTION: How did Ruth react to Boaz's kind words?

ANSWER: Verse 10 tells us that "[Ruth] prostrated herself with her face to the ground, and said to [Boaz]: 'Why are you so kind as to single me out, when I am a foreigner?'" Overwhelmed by Boaz's benevolence, Ruth bowed down before him. Knowing the controversy associated with Moabite converts, Ruth could hardly believe Boaz's warm welcome; knowing of the Moabite reputation for immoral behavior, she found it hard to fathom that Boaz could think highly of her and was astounded by the many courtesies Boaz extended.

———

QUESTION: In what way is the Jewish tradition of kindness the opposite of the Moabite approach?

ANSWER: Abraham, the first Hebrew, embodied kindness, as myriad examples in *Genesis* make clear. For example, he warmly welcomed and prepared a feast for three travelers who passed his way though he, himself, was recovering from circumcision; and when he was told by those wayfarers that God was going to destroy Sodom and Gomorrah, he bargained with God to spare the inhabitants of those evil cities (*Genesis* 18).

The Moabites were just the opposite—a stingy and mean-spirited lot—as we discussed in chapter 1. The Rambam says that a person who throws a thousand dinars to one who is poor, but insults him or her, has not fulfilled the mitzvah of charity.[47]

Asking for charity can be embarrassing; Jewish law forbids humiliating the impoverished. If a poor person knocks at your door and you give him fifty dollars, but you are so insolent that he will never dare ask you for anything again, you have committed a sin. When you give, Judaism teaches, give the best that you are able; don't just give the poor throwaway items or items in disrepair. Even a person who has no money to give but who is willing to sit and listen to the poor and to encourage him or her can fulfill the mitzvah of charity.

———

QUESTION: The Torah records several shameful incidents involving the Moabites. What was the first?

ANSWER: After God saved Lot and his daughters from the destruction of the cities of Sodom and Gomorrah (*Genesis* 19), the three fled to the mountains. Believing that they were the world's only survivors, Lot's daughters got him drunk and had sexual relations with him in the hope of producing offspring. Each daughter bore a son, one named Moab, the other Ben-ammi, who became the fathers of the Moabite and Ammonite nations, respectively.

———

QUESTION: Didn't Lot's daughters act with good motive?

ANSWER: Possibly, in that they thought they and their father were the only people left on earth, but their behavior lacked all modesty. Indeed, Lot's older daughter named her son Moab, which means "from my father," making no attempt to conceal the special circumstances surrounding the birth of her son. She might even have been proud of the situation. Lot's younger daughter named her son Ben-ammi, which means "son of my people," also alluding to the circumstances of the birth of her child, but in a much more subtle manner.

———

QUESTION: How did this incident affect the relationship between Moab and the Israelites?

ANSWER: It created a permanent barrier between the two peoples. Abraham no longer wished to have any association with his nephew Lot. This incident certainly was not in keeping with the ideals of the Jewish people that Abraham was about to establish.

———

QUESTION: What was the second shameful incident involving the Moabites?

ANSWER: Balak, King of Moab, hired the soothsayer Balaam to curse the Israelites while they camped in Moabite territory on their way to the Promised Land. Such a curse, the Moabites believed, would allow them to annihilate the Jews. It was only through divine intervention that the curse was changed into a blessing (*Numbers* 22–24).

———

QUESTION: What was the third incident?

ANSWER: Unable to curse the Israelites, Balaam advised Balak to lure the Israelites into immoral behavior, which would enrage God and cause God to sever his special relationship with the Israelites. In order to achieve his evil goal, Balak did not hesitate to use young girls from his own country as bait to lead the Israelites into sin (*Numbers* 25:1, *Deuteronomy* 23:4–5).

—

QUESTION: What was the fourth incident?

ANSWER: At the end of the Israelites' forty-year journey in the desert, just as they were about to enter the Land of Israel, they asked the Moabites to permit them to cross through their land, promising to make it worth their while by buying food from them and boosting their economy. Moab refused them not only the right of passage but even the opportunity to buy food (*Deuteronomy* 23:4–5).

—

QUESTION: Did the Israelites ever take revenge against the Moabites?

ANSWER: No. After all, the Moabites, descendents of Lot, nephew of Abraham, were their cousins. However, the Moabite nation was such a wicked one that the Torah forbade Jewish women to marry Moabite men.

—

QUESTION: How did Boaz respond when Ruth prostrated herself before him?

ANSWER: Boaz answered, "I have been told of all that you did for your mother-in-law after the death of your husband, how you left your father and mother and the land of your birth and came to a people you had not known before" (2:11). The shameful history of the country of her birth had no bearing on Boaz's opinion of her. Boaz was moved by the kindness she extended Naomi, and he admired the fact that she had abandoned everything to join the Israelite nation. He accepted her on her own merits. If she thought she would not be able to marry into the Israelite nation when she converted to Judaism, her conversion was all the more commendable.

———

QUESTION: Why did Boaz repeat the words "I have been told" in verse 11: *huged hugad*?

ANSWER: Boaz answered both of Ruth's unspoken questions. The first "I have been told," *huged*, is in response to Ruth's understanding that she was not permitted to marry an Israelite. On the contrary, Boaz indicated, she *was* permitted to marry an Israelite.

The Sages say that three days before the meeting between Boaz and Ruth, a huge debate erupted in the high court about whether the prohibition against Israelites marrying Moabite converts applied to all Moabites or

only male Moabite converts. It was decided that Israelite men would be permitted to marry female Moabite
converts, but that Israelite women could not marry male
Moabite converts. Boaz not only served on the Sanhedrin but was its head. Still, he modestly indicated that
Ruth would be permitted to marry an Israelite.[48]

QUESTION: What is the meaning of Boaz's second "I
have been told"—*hugad*?

ANSWER: Boaz conveyed to Ruth that he had received an inspiration, a prophetic dream about her, in
which it was revealed that she was an exceptional woman who would merit bringing a future redeemer (King
David) into the world.[49]

QUESTION: What did Boaz do next?

ANSWER: Boaz blessed Ruth: "May the Lord reward
your deeds. May you have a full recompense from the
Lord, the God of Israel, under whose wings you have
sought refuge!" (2:12). In other words, Ruth's character
and deeds were so great that no person could reward her
properly. She achieved a spiritual level unparalleled by
others. Her reward—the future redeemer, King David—
would be sent by God. King David, in turn, would inherit
Ruth's all-consuming faith. Even when he was surround-
ed by enemies, even though one of his sons would rebel
against him, his faith in God would not waver.

QUESTION: What other reward did Ruth merit from God?

ANSWER: Ruth lived a very long life, witnessing not only King David's rule but the building of the First Temple by King Solomon, her great-great-grandson.[50]

———

QUESTION: Is there another explanation for the double blessing Boaz bestowed upon Ruth: "May the Lord reward your deeds" and "May you have a full recompense from the Lord, the God of Israel, under whose wings you have sought refuge"?

ANSWER: The first part of the blessing corresponds to the earthly world, where rewards are given but not necessarily in full. The second part of the blessing refers to the rewards that await the righteous in the world to come.[51]

———

QUESTION: According to the Sages, Boaz had a vision about Ruth. What was it?

ANSWER: Boaz told her that while, in her present circumstances, she may be on a low rung of the social and economic ladder, he could foresee that one day she would rise to the top of the ladder. In his vision, she was wearing the clothes of royalty, indicating that her descendants would become leaders and kings of Israel.[52]

———

QUESTION: Was Boaz a prophet?

ANSWER: Boaz was not recognized as a prophet, but he clearly possessed prophetic ability and intuition.

———

QUESTION: How did Boaz's blessing make Ruth feel?

ANSWER: She was completely assuaged: "You are most kind, my lord, to comfort me and to speak gently to your maidservant—though I am not so much as one of your maidservants" (2:13). She did not prostrate herself again because she was no longer embarrassed. She knew that there were people like Boaz who would accept her no matter where she came from.

———

QUESTION: In verse 14, Boaz invited Ruth to, "Come over here and partake of the meal, and dip your morsel in the vinegar." What did he mean by this?

ANSWER: Boaz not only invited Ruth to help herself to water if she was thirsty, but later in the day, at mealtime, he invited her to eat with him and his harvesters.

———

QUESTION: Verses 8 through 14 record the many courtesies Boaz extended to Ruth. What were they?

ANSWER:

1. He called her *biti*, my daughter.
2. He told her to stay in his field and glean.
3. He assured her his men would not molest her.
4. He invited her to help herself to water.
5. He complimented her on all that she had done to help Naomi and on her conversion.
6. He asked that God bless and reward her.
7. He invited her to join him and his harvesters for a meal.

QUESTION: Why did Boaz take these steps?

ANSWER: Boaz was a man who paid attention to every detail. He knew that Ruth had suffered many difficulties, that she was embarrassed about having to ask for charity, that as a Moabite she was unsure about how she would be received by the townspeople of Bethlehem, and Boaz in particular, since she was picking barley in his field. Each of the small steps Boaz took was designed to elevate her comfort level and raise her self-esteem.

One may compare Boaz's gradual approach to the way in which God prepared Abraham for the binding of Isaac: "Take your son, your only son, the one whom you love, Isaac…"

QUESTION: Boaz not only offered Ruth food in verse 14, but he did something more personal. What was it?

ANSWER: Boaz handed Ruth the food—toasted grain—himself. He could have delegated the job of serving Ruth to one of his field hands, but instead he served her personally, the highest expression of kindness and true caring.

QUESTION: The way in which Boaz served Ruth, a stranger in his field, is reminiscent of the story in *Genesis*, mentioned above, of Abraham and the three angels. What are the similarities between the two stories?

ANSWER: *Genesis* 18 recounts how Abraham, a few short days after being circumcised, was resting at the entrance to his tent in the heat of the day when three men (actually angels sent by God) approached. Abraham hurried out of his tent to greet them, bowed down to the ground, and said, "If I have found favor in your sight, please stay here...wash your feet [which are dusty from the road], rest under the tree. I will get you a morsel of bread." Then Abraham hurried to his wife, Sarah, and asked her to bake cakes while he had one of his servants butcher a calf. When the meal was ready, Abraham served it to his guests.

Similarly, Boaz welcomed Ruth to his field, and asked her to stay and glean in it. He invited her to help herself to water, and at mealtime, he, himself, gave her food.

QUESTION: Did Boaz feed Ruth out of consideration for her or to ease his guilty conscience?

ANSWER: Boaz honored Ruth by serving her personally. This is another example of Boaz's great generosity and teaches that if a person performs a good deed, he or she should do it wholeheartedly.

QUESTION: Why does verse 14 describe at length the meal prepared by Boaz that Ruth ate?

ANSWER: This was the first satisfying meal that Ruth had eaten in a long time. She savored every bite.

QUESTION: Of what did the meal consist?

ANSWER: The meal was quite frugal: bread, vinegar, in which to dip the bread, and toasted grain.

QUESTION: Didn't they have anything better to eat?

ANSWER: They surely did, but not in the fields. It also is important to remember that Israel had only recently emerged from a severe drought, and a simple meal of bread, vinegar, and grain may have felt like a feast.

QUESTION: Why did they dip their bread in vinegar?

ANSWER: Vinegar is a thirst-quencher. Having worked in the sun for many hours, the harvesters must have been quite hot and thirsty. Bread dipped in vinegar was cooling.

———

QUESTION: Is there another explanation?

ANSWER: Some say the word *chometz*, which we usually translate as "vinegar," actually refers to a special dish made with vinegar. It was as if Boaz were saying to Ruth: "Dip your bread in this delectable dish."

———

QUESTION: Verse 14 tells us that Ruth "ate her fill and had some left over." What is significant about that?

ANSWER: The Talmud promotes healthy eating and teaches that a person should not leave the table so full that he or she feels ill. The Sages base their advice—to eat in moderation—in part, on verse 14 of the *Book of Ruth*. Though Ruth was hungry when she sat down, she was careful not to eat to excess and so left over a portion of the grain.[53]

We learn another lesson from the abundance of grain Ruth was served, that of *berakhah be-isah* (*berakhah* means "blessing" and *isah* "dough"). When one mixes up dough, one never knows exactly how much the dough will rise or how much bread it will make—sometimes the blessing is much greater than anticipated. As the *Book of Ruth* unfolds, the blessings that God showered on Ruth and Boaz were as numerous as they were unexpected.

——

QUESTION: Did Ruth return to work after the meal, or was she confident that Boaz would take care of her, deeming it unnecessary for her to continue picking the leftover stalks?

ANSWER: Not only did Ruth continue working in the field, but the Sages say that Ruth was the very first to finish her meal and return to work. She was not one to waste time.

——

QUESTION: When Ruth got up to return to the field, what did Boaz instruct his workers to do?

ANSWER: Boaz made it clear to his workers that Ruth was permitted to gather grain anywhere she wanted, with no questions asked (2:15).

——

QUESTION: Was that all?

ANSWER: No. Boaz instructed his workers to deliberately pull out stalks from the sheaves for her to gather (2:17). Above all, Boaz exhorted his workers not to scold or rebuke her.

——

QUESTION: How long did Ruth continue gleaning in the field?

ANSWER: Ruth gleaned in the field until evening, we are told in verse 17. Although she knew she had found favor in Boaz's eyes, she was an extremely hard worker.

———

QUESTION: How much grain did Ruth gather?

ANSWER: Ruth gathered approximately one *eifah* of grain, quite a large amount.[54]

———

QUESTION: How much is an *eifah*?

ANSWER: One *eifah* equals about ten *omers*. A single *omer* is enough to feed one person for one day, therefore, Ruth gathered enough to feed herself and Naomi for five days.[55]

———

QUESTION: What did Ruth do with all the barley she collected?

ANSWER: She immediately took it home to her mother-in-law, Naomi.

———

QUESTION: How was Ruth able to carry home so much barley?

ANSWER: The text tells us that she beat it out, in other words, she separated the grain from the stalks.

QUESTION: Why does verse 18 say, "...her mother-in-law [Naomi] saw what she [Ruth] had gleaned"?

ANSWER: This indicates that Ruth—ever modest—did not brag about the amount of grain she had gathered. Rather Naomi saw the copious quantity and was astonished by it.

QUESTION: The last line of verse 18 reads that she "took out and gave her what she had left over after eating her fill." To whom does this refer?

ANSWER: It would seem out of character for Ruth to take first. It is likely that Ruth offered the grain to Naomi, and then, when Naomi was finished eating, she offered the rest to Ruth.

QUESTION: After Ruth and Naomi ate, Naomi asked Ruth, "Where did you glean today? Where did you work?" (2:19). What information was Naomi trying to elicit?

ANSWER: Amazed by the amount of grain Ruth brought home, a number of questions occurred to Naomi: Where had Ruth found a field owned by such a generous individual? How was Ruth able in a single day to gather so much grain? If, as some commentators say, Ruth not only brought home grain but leftovers from lunch, how had she had time to eat when she was so busy gathering up the grain? Landowners didn't usually allow gleaners to beat stalks in the field; which land-owner was kind enough to allow Ruth to do so?

QUESTION: Naomi said about Ruth's benefactor, "Blessed be he who took such generous notice of you!" (2:19) What did she mean by this?

ANSWER: Naomi hoped that the owner of the field in which Ruth had gleaned was as goodhearted as he seemed and motivated by honorable intentions; she prayed her words would make it so.

QUESTION: How did Ruth respond to Naomi?

ANSWER: According to the Sages, Ruth modestly told Naomi that she had done nothing extraordinary (though we know it was divine providence), but had happened to come to the right field, where the owner was very kind to her and helped her gather all that she had brought home. Ruth reassured Naomi that she had not taken anything that another poor widow would not have been able to gather. Despite the fact that the landowner told his workers to let her take whatever she wanted, she did not take advantage of him.[56]

QUESTION: When did Ruth reveal the name of the man in whose field she had gleaned?

ANSWER: Only at the end of verse 19 does Ruth say, "The name of the man with whom I worked today is Boaz."

———

QUESTION: The Sages learn a profound lesson from the prophet Samuel's choice of the words *asher asiti imo*— "with whom I worked"—over *asher asah imadi*—"who has worked [helped] with me." What is that lesson?

ANSWER: According to the Sages, it costs a wealthy man nothing to give a poor man a piece of bread. The poor person's deed is greater—it is he who provides the wealthy the opportunity to give and who brings God's gratitude and blessing to the rich. The phrase "who has worked with me" would indicate that Boaz made the greater sacrifice; "with whom I worked" indicates that it was only on account of Ruth that Boaz merited a reward.[57]

———

QUESTION: The root of the word *asiti*—*asah*—means "do." Is there another interpretation for the phrase *asher asiti imo*?

ANSWER: Yes. Some commentators suggest that by sharing her story with him, what Ruth did for Boaz was bring him solace after the sorrow he had experienced upon the death of his wife.[58]

———

QUESTION: What did Naomi say in answer to Ruth's statement that it was Boaz's field in which she had gleaned?

ANSWER: First, Naomi blessed him—"Blessed be he of the Lord, who has not failed in His kindness to the living or to the dead!"—and only then did she reveal to Ruth that Boaz was closely related to them, one of their "redeeming kinsmen" (2:20).

———

QUESTION: Why did Naomi say "Blessed be he of the Lord"?

ANSWER: Naomi understood that although she and Ruth were indebted to Boaz, they were in no position to repay his kindness. Naomi was convinced, however, that God would reward Boaz handsomely for his benevolence.

———

QUESTION: Why didn't Naomi immediately reveal to Ruth that Boaz was their relative?

ANSWER: Naomi cleverly hid the fact that Boaz was related to them so that Ruth would not think this was Naomi's reason for blessing him. Boaz deserved Naomi's blessing because of the great deeds he had performed, not because they were relatives.

———

QUESTION: If a husband dies childless, does the Torah make any provision to insure that his memory will be perpetuated and his property remain within the family?

ANSWER: Yes. *Deuteronomy* 25:5–6 delineates the procedure of levirate marriage—in Hebrew, *yibbum*—by which the brother of a deceased, childless man is encouraged to marry his widow and produce an heir who will carry the deceased man's name (in Hebrew, perpetuating the name of the deceased is referred to as *meshiv nefesh*, literally, "returning the soul") and inherit his property. Though *Leviticus* 18:16 prohibits a brother from marrying his sister-in-law under any other circumstances, the perpetuation of the deceased brother's name is considered so critical that this exception is made.

———

QUESTION: What if the deceased's brother does not wish to marry his widow?

ANSWER: The Torah provides for this situation as well (*Deuteronomy* 25:7–10). If the brother does not wish to marry the widow, the *chalitzah* ceremony must take place before the widow can marry somebody else. To perform *chalitzah*, the widow takes a special *chalitzah* shoe from her brother-in-law's foot and spits on the ground in front of him as an indication of her disdain for his refusal to help perpetuate her husband's name. The *chalitzah* ceremony must take place in front of the town elders.

———

QUESTION: Would levirate marriage have been applicable in Ruth's situation?

ANSWER: There are several schools of thought regarding the interpretation of the term "redeeming kinsmen" and its applicability to levirate marriage, including those of Rashi, Ibn Ezra, and the Ramban.

———

QUESTION: How did Rashi interpret the phrase "redeeming kinsman"?

ANSWER: Rashi favored a simple or literal translation of the text. He believed that Ruth simply wanted to get married and that Naomi indicated to her that Boaz, a relative, was a prospective husband.[59]

———

QUESTION: How did the great twelfth-century, Spanish Bible commentator and poet Abraham Ibn Ezra interpret the term "redeeming kinsman"?

ANSWER: Ibn Ezra believed that the word *redemption* in "redeeming kinsman" referred only to the redemption of property—in this case, the property, specifically real estate, that had belonged to Elimelech, for which Naomi and Ruth were now responsible.[60]

———

QUESTION: How would the Jewish laws of inheritance have been applied to Elimelech's survivors?

ANSWER: According to the laws of inheritance (*Numbers* 27:6–11, *Deuteronomy* 21:17), if a father dies, his sons would inherit his property, with a double portion going to the older son. If a man dies leaving only daughters, the daughters inherit his property. If a man dies childless, his brothers or the next closest male relatives inherit his property.

When a Jewish woman marries, she receives a *ketubbah,* a legal document outlining her husband's obligations to her, including provisions, often monetary, in case of death or divorce. According to Ibn Ezra, Elimelech did not leave Naomi money when he died, but an actual portion of his property. Also according to Ibn Ezra, Ruth had converted or had begun the process of conversion before she married Mahlon. Her *ketubbah* stated that, upon his death, she would inherit Mahlon's property, but only if she married his closest relative.[61]

QUESTION: What does the Torah say about the redemption of property?

ANSWER: *Leviticus* 25:25–28 states that if a man becomes impoverished and is forced to sell his land or possessions, the property should be redeemed by a kinsman. In other words, the nearest kinsman is offered the property first for purchase.

QUESTION: How did Moses Nahmanides, the thirteenth-century biblical scholar and kabbalist known as the Ramban (not to be confused with Maimonides, the Rambam), interpret the phrase "redeeming kinsman"?

ANSWER: According to the Ramban and other scholars, levirate marriage was not limited to the brother of a man who died childless but could be performed by any close male relative. Thus, when Naomi used the term "redeeming kinsman" in verse 20, she was referring to the obligation of Boaz (or any other close relative of Elimelech, Mahlon, and Chilion) to marry Ruth and perpetuate the name of Ruth's husband, Mahlon.[62]

QUESTION: The Ramban offers a more mystical interpretation of levirate marriage, as well. What is it?

ANSWER: Unlike Rashi, who favored a literal approach to the Scriptures, or Maimonides, a philosopher in the Aristotelian mold, Nahmanides believed in delving deep beneath the surface of the Torah text to extract its esoteric meaning. The Ramban was one of the earliest scholars to teach the concept of the transmigration of souls, the passage, after death, of a broken soul, a soul in need of *tikkun*—repair—into a new body. According to the Ramban, the birth of Obed, son of Ruth and Boaz, as a result of levirate marriage, represented the reincarnation of Mahlon's soul into its new home.

QUESTION: Is the *Book of Ruth* the first example of the transmigration of souls in Scriptures?

ANSWER: No. According to the Ramban, the first recorded example of the transmigration of souls appears in *Genesis* 38, which recounts the story of Judah (fourth son of the patriarch Jacob) and his daughter-in-law, Tamar. Tamar was married to Judah's oldest son, Er. Er was "displeasing to the Lord, and the Lord took his life" (*Genesis* 38:7; the Sages say Er married Tamar because of her great beauty but refused to have children with her). Because Er did not have children, Judah married Tamar to his second oldest son, Onan, but Onan, "knowing that the seed would not count as his, let it go to waste whenever he joined with his brother's wife, so as not to provide offspring for his brother" (*Genesis* 38:9). This, too, was displeasing to God, and God took Onan's life. Judah then promised Tamar that his youngest son, Shelah, would marry her when he grew up, so Tamar returned to her father's house to wait. Years went by, and Shelah grew up, but Judah did not arrange for his youngest son to marry Tamar. When Tamar learned that Judah's wife had died and that Judah was coming to shear sheep in Timnah, she disguised herself as a harlot and waited for Judah at the entrance to the town of Enaim. Judah, not realizing that the "harlot" was Tamar, had intimate relations with her. Afterward, Tamar asked Judah to leave a pledge with her until he could send her a sheep in payment for her services; he left his seal, cord, and staff.

When he sent a servant to pay Tamar as promised, the servant was unable to locate her.

A few months later, Judah became incensed when he learned that Tamar was pregnant. "Bring her out," said Judah, "and let her be burned." As Tamar was being led out, she sent a message to her father-in-law: "I am with child by the man to whom these [seal, cord, and staff] belong." When Judah recognized these objects as his own, he said, "She is more in the right than I, inasmuch as I did not give her to my son Shelah" (*Genesis* 38:24–26).

Tamar would go on to give birth to twins, Perez and Zerah. According to the Ramban's interpretation of this story about levirate marriage, Perez was Er reincarnated. Furthermore, Boaz is a direct descendant of Perez!

———

QUESTION: Are there other rabbis who shared the Ramban's belief in the transmigration of souls?

ANSWER: Yes. The nineteenth-century biblical commentator Rabbi Me'ir Leibush Malbim,* who served as the chief rabbi of Bucharest and then as the chief rabbi of Romania, interpreted the term "redeeming kinsman" similarly to the Ramban.

———

---

* The Malbim was a disciple of my great-grandfather, Tzvi Hirsch of Zhidachov.

QUESTION: After Ruth learned from Naomi that Boaz was a redeeming kinsman, what did she tell Naomi in verse 21?

ANSWER: Ruth told Naomi that Boaz had told her to remain with his workers until the end of the harvest season.

———

QUESTION: Why did Ruth wait until after Naomi revealed that Boaz was a redeemer to tell Naomi that Boaz had invited her to remain with his workers until the end of the harvest?

ANSWER: Ruth was concerned that Naomi would be suspicious of Boaz's motives in inviting Ruth to remain in his fields until the end of the harvest season. Knowing that Boaz was a redeeming kinsman allayed Ruth's doubts.

———

QUESTION: In verse 8, Boaz had directed Ruth to stay close to his "girls," *na'arot*. However, when Ruth told Naomi that Boaz had instructed her to "stay close by my workers" (2:21), she uses the masculine form of the word, *ne'arim*. Naomi responds to Ruth, "It is best, daughter, that you go out with [Boaz's] girls," *na'arot*. Is the inconsistency in language significant?

ANSWER: It most certainly is. The *Book of Ruth* was recorded by the prophet Samuel. Since it was divinely inspired, every nuance must be carefully examined.

———

QUESTION: Did Ruth misunderstand Boaz's advice?

ANSWER: Possibly. As the product of a lascivious culture, Ruth may have misinterpreted Boaz's words. Perhaps that is why verse 21 reminds us again of her Moabite origins.[63] Or the confusion may be attributed to the fact that Hebrew was not Ruth's first language; therefore, she did not know the difference between masculine and feminine forms and so confused *ne'arim* (masculine) with *na'arot* (feminine). This explanation is more appealing when one considers Ruth's modest nature.[64"]

———

QUESTION: Why did Naomi correct Ruth?

ANSWER: Knowing what a conscientious man Boaz was, Naomi may not have had serious concerns about the intentions of Boaz's male workers. However, for the sake of propriety, Naomi advised Ruth to stick with the female workers.

———

QUESTION: In verse 22, Naomi advised Ruth to stick closely to Boaz's female workers so that she would "not be annoyed in some other field." Why did she add this proviso?

ANSWER: Naomi feared that Ruth would receive unwanted advances from workers in other fields. She also hoped that Boaz and Ruth would become better acquainted and so did not wish Ruth to glean in fields belonging to anybody but Boaz.

———

QUESTION: Why does Naomi refer to Ruth as both *kallatah*, her "daughter-in-law," and *biti*, "my daughter," in verse 22?

ANSWER: This is another expression of Naomi's deep feelings for Ruth. Naomi looked upon Ruth as her own daughter, not just a daughter-in-law.

———

QUESTION: How does chapter 2 conclude?

ANSWER: We learn from verse 23, the last verse of chapter 2, that Ruth heeded her mother-in-law's advice and stayed close to Boaz's female harvesters until the end not only of the barley harvest but the wheat harvest as well.

———

QUESTION: How long a period of time was this?

ANSWER: Ruth remained with the harvesters for three months, the duration of the harvest season.

———

QUESTION: What did Ruth do when the harvest season was over?

ANSWER: Some commentators say that Ruth lived with Boaz's workers during the entire harvest period, bringing food to Naomi but returning to live with Naomi only at the end of the harvest season. Other commentators say that Ruth returned to Naomi every night, bringing food and keeping Naomi company.[65]

———

QUESTION: Is there anything else significant about the three-month period?

ANSWER: Jewish law requires a widow to wait three months before remarrying, in case she is pregnant with her deceased husband's child. By the end of the three-month harvest season, it was clear that Ruth was not pregnant, and her relationship with Boaz could move to a new level.[66]

Chapter 3

Synopsis

Concerned about Ruth's security and Elimelech's legacy, Naomi reveals her hopes that Ruth and Boaz will marry and produce an heir, and instructs Ruth about how she should approach Boaz. That night, Ruth goes down to the threshing floor where Boaz is sleeping; he is startled to wake up and find Ruth lying at his feet! Though he is eager to redeem her, he reveals to Ruth that there is a male relative even more closely related to Ruth and Naomi than he and that this other relative must be consulted before Boaz can act. Ruth returns to Naomi with a gift of grain from Boaz, and Naomi counsels Ruth to wait patiently until Boaz has attended to matters.

———

QUESTION: Chapter 2 closes with the end of the harvest season. How does chapter 3 open?

ANSWER: Because there was nothing left to harvest in the fields, Naomi remarked to Ruth that she had to find security for her, "where you may be happy" (3:1). In other words, Naomi intended to find Ruth a new husband and a new home, befitting Ruth's worth and character.

QUESTION: Why did Naomi take it upon herself to engineer the union of Ruth and Boaz?

ANSWER: Before Naomi died, she wanted to secure Elimelech's property in Bethlehem and ensure the continuation of Elimelech's line. In order to do this, Ruth would have to marry and have a child. Although Naomi hoped that Boaz would marry Ruth, Boaz had not yet made any move to make Ruth his wife—even though Ruth's conversion to Judaism had taken place at least three months before, at the beginning of the harvest season (and according to the Ramban, as we discussed in chapter 2, Ruth had begun the conversion process even before she married Mahlon). Therefore, Naomi instructed Ruth in a straightforward, honest, yet gentle, manner about how she might approach Boaz.

———

QUESTION: Why is it significant that Naomi calls Ruth her "daughter" in verse 1?

ANSWER: Might not a mother whose married son has died begrudge the remarriage of her daughter-in-law? Not Naomi! She regarded Ruth as her daughter and only wanted what was best for her: the happiness and security that a new marriage would ensure. This evokes the blessing that Naomi had given Ruth and Orpah in chapter 1, verse 9, when she urged her daughters-in-law to return to their homes: "May the Lord grant that each of you find security in the house of a husband."[1]

———

QUESTION: What was significant about Naomi's choice of words, *mano'ach*—"home" or "security"?

ANSWER: When a man and woman marry, their union creates a secure space, a sanctuary of peace: "For a man has no peace without a wife, nor a woman without a husband."[2] This is what Naomi wished for Ruth, that she would remarry and that her new union, her new home, would offer her security and serenity. *Mano'ach* is the same word that Naomi used in chapter 1, verse 9, when she encouraged her daughters-in-law to return to their people, find new mates, and enjoy marital bliss.[3] In addition to security, Naomi prayed that Ruth would reap spiritual satisfaction—*nachat ru'ach*; the word *nachat* shares the same Hebrew root as *mano'ach: nun-vav-chet*.

———

QUESTION: To what else does the word *mano'ach* allude?

ANSWER: Some commentators point out that the word *mano'ach* is an allusion to King Solomon, son of David, and great-great-grandson of Ruth and Boaz, whose reign was one of peace and who built the First Temple—the Beit ha-Mikdash—as an earthly resting place for the Divine Presence (the *Shekhinah*): "Now the Lord my God has given me respite [*heni'ach*] all around; there is no adversary and no mischance. And so I propose to build a house for the name of the Lord my God, as the Lord promised my father David..."

(*1 Kings* 5:18–19). Another word that shares the same root as *mano'ach* is *menachem,* "the comforter," another name for the Messiah, who, as the Torah teaches, will come from the house of David.[4]

———

QUESTION: In addition to a sense of security, what are some of the other ideals of Jewish marriage?

ANSWER: In chapters 1 and 2 we discussed the story of Eliezer, trusted servant of Abraham, who set out to find a wife for Abraham's son, Isaac. Eliezer knew that he would recognize the woman intended for Isaac by her kindness and compassion: when he asked Rebekah, who had come to the well to draw water, for a drink, she not only offered to give him water but his camels as well (*Genesis* 24:43–44). Kindness, compassion, and affection are the hallmarks of a good marriage, and surely traits that attracted Boaz and Ruth to each other. A Jewish marriage, built on these qualities and the foundation of Torah and mitzvot, is called a *binyan adei ad*—"an everlasting edifice." *Genesis* 2:22 describes God's creation of Eve with the word *va-yiven,* which means to "build." The Talmud teaches that God blessed Adam and Eve by erecting ten canopies—*chuppot*—for them in the Garden of Eden.[5] Today, the *chuppah* under which the bride and groom stand during a Jewish wedding ceremony symbolizes the home they will build together.

———

QUESTION: What did Naomi propose that Ruth do?

ANSWER: Naomi encouraged Ruth to go back to the threshing floor and seek out Boaz.

———

QUESTION: Ruth was quite familiar with Boaz. Why did Naomi remind Ruth that he was their relative, with whose girls she had picked grain (3:2)?

ANSWER: Afraid that Ruth would respond negatively to Naomi's suggestion that she go down to the threshing floor, Naomi subtly reminded Ruth of Boaz's qualities: that he was well-known and respected, a relative of their family, and a generous, righteous man, as Ruth knew because she had worked with his girls in the fields.

———

QUESTION: Naomi had explained to Ruth at the beginning of the harvest season that Boaz was a redeeming kinsman, and we are told that Ruth gleaned in Boaz's fields with his girls until the barley and wheat harvests were finished. During this three-month period, do we have any indication that Boaz intimated that he was willing to redeem Ruth?

ANSWER: No. Boaz, according to the Sages, was an eighty-year-old man who had experienced much sorrow during his lifetime. It did not occur to him to redeem Ruth, even though, according to the commentators, he was interested. Although he was willing to take certain initiatives—making sure that Ruth was able to collect enough grain to feed herself and her mother-in-law, making sure that she was not harassed in the fields while doing so—that was as far as he would go.[6]

QUESTION: What troubles had befallen Boaz in his lifetime?

ANSWER: According to the Midrash, Boaz's wife had died at the very same time that Naomi and Ruth had arrived in Bethlehem. It is said that Boaz had thirty sons and thirty daughters, all of whom had died earlier. Under the circumstances, Boaz felt hopeless. He couldn't conceive of starting from scratch at age eighty and building a new home with Ruth, comparatively a young woman. Moreover, as we will learn later in the chapter, there was a redeeming kinsmen more closely related to Naomi and Ruth than Boaz.[7]

QUESTION: So did it seem too much to expect Boaz to marry Ruth?

ANSWER: Absolutely. If, as the Midrash says, Boaz was eighty years old, it is unlikely he would feel up to assuming the burden of two destitute women or the further responsibilities of farming their land. In addition, at his advanced age, there was every chance that Ruth would become a widow shortly after marrying him.

QUESTION: Was Ruth willing to fulfill Naomi's wishes and go to Boaz that night (3:3–5)?

ANSWER: In another exceptional act of kindness, Ruth suppressed her personal feelings and desires, and, putting her trust in Naomi as she had done all along, abided by her mother-in-law's wishes.

———

QUESTION: What did Naomi instruct Ruth to do and why?

ANSWER: Naomi told Ruth to "bathe" and "anoint" herself (3:3). According to some commentators, on special occasions, such as the Sabbath or Jewish holidays, nobles would bathe and perfume themselves, and dress in their best clothing; according to other commentators, Naomi's instructions referred to immersion in a mikvah—a "ritual bath."[8]

———

QUESTION: How old is the practice of ritual immersion and is it still practiced today?

ANSWER: After the complete cessation of monthly menstruation, married women are required to wait seven "clean" days and then immerse themselves in a mikvah. Prior to engaging in intimate relations, it also is traditional for a Jewish bride to immerse herself in a mikvah.

In fact, immersion in a mikvah is a ritual that has been practiced since the beginning of Creation. The Sages teach that when Adam and Eve were banished from Paradise, Adam, as a sign of repentance, immersed himself in a river that flowed from the Garden of Eden. In preparation for receiving the Torah at Mount Sinai, God instructed the Israelites to stay pure and wash their clothes (*Exodus* 19:10, 14); many commentators understand this to mean that the Israelites ritually immersed themselves. So, too, the famous "well of Miriam," which accompanied the Jews in the desert following the Exodus from Egypt, is thought to have been a ritual bath. Immersion in a mikvah is strongly connected to the priesthood: Aaron and his sons ritually immersed themselves before assuming the priesthood; later, priests—in fact, all worshipers, male and female—immersed themselves before entering the Temple, and on Yom Kippur, the high priest was required to immerse himself in a ritual bath before he could enter the Holy of Holies. Archaeologists digging along the southern side of the Temple site in Jerusalem have uncovered the remains of numerous mikvahs.[9]

QUESTION: Many commentators interpret Naomi's instructions in a more mystical fashion. Why do they believe Naomi instructed Ruth to bathe before going back to Boaz's fields?

ANSWER: They believe Naomi instructed Ruth to immerse herself in a mikvah as a symbolic purging of the idolatrous influences of Moab. In addition, some say that Naomi told Ruth to immerse herself in the mikvah because she believed that the unredeemed spirit of Mahlon—her son and Ruth's husband—clung to Ruth.[10]

―――

QUESTION: Why was Mahlon's soul unable to rest?

ANSWER: Because of his great sin—marrying one of the daughters of the king of Moab—Mahlon's spirit was unsettled. Some commentators add that Mahlon's soul was unable to rest because he died childless. In order to move on with her life, Ruth's body had to be released from Mahlon's spirit, which could be achieved, in part, by immersion in a ritual bath.[11]

―――

QUESTION: From where does this supernatural interpretation come?

ANSWER: In the mystical writings of the Zohar, it says that the spirit of a woman's first husband stays with her until it is replaced by the spirit of a new husband.

―――

QUESTION: In addition to bathing and anointing herself, Naomi also instructed Ruth to "dress up" (3:3). Why?

ANSWER: Naomi urged Ruth to prepare for her mission—that of persuading Boaz to redeem her—as one prepares for the holy Sabbath: by bathing, anointing herself, and donning her finest attire.[12]

QUESTION: There are several instances in which the public reading of the *Book of Ruth* differs from the written text. What is this called?

ANSWER: *Keri*—"what is read [aloud in the Scriptures by the public reader in synagogue that differs from what is written in the text]"—and *ketiv*—"what is written [in the Scriptures that differs from the public reading of the text]."

QUESTION: How many instances are there of *keri* and *ketiv* in the Tanakh and why?

ANSWER: There are numerous examples of *keri* and *ketiv* in the Tanakh. Religious Jews believe that even these variations between the written word and the spoken word come directly from God and that each teaches a specific lesson.

QUESTION: Why did Naomi tell Ruth to "go down" to the threshing floor (3:3)?

ANSWER: The simple explanation is that the threshing floor was located below the city. However, the presence of the letter *yud* that appears at the end of the word *ve-yaradet* (but that is not pronounced when the *Book of Ruth* is read aloud), which changes the meaning of the word from "go down" to "I will go down," has been interpreted in the Midrash to mean "my prayers will descend with you." In other words, Naomi told Ruth that she would be with Ruth in spirit when Ruth went down to Boaz on the threshing floor.

———

QUESTION: Are there other explanations of the word *va-yaradet*?

ANSWER: Ruth was the daughter of a king, yet she was willing to lower herself and lie at Boaz's feet in order to get Boaz to redeem her. Ruth's self-abasement reminds us of Jonah praying to God from the belly of the great fish (*Jonah* 2) or *Psalm* 130, which begins: "Out of the depths I call to you, O Lord."

———

QUESTION: It seems clear from Naomi's instructions to Ruth in verses 3 and 4—to bathe and to dress herself in her finest clothing, to sneak down to the threshing floor, and to lie down at Boaz's feet—that Naomi wants Ruth to entice Boaz. What did Naomi have in mind?

ANSWER: Naomi sees in Ruth a woman with her whole life still ahead of her, including marriage and children. Yet Ruth is no closer to fulfilling Naomi's hopes than she was when she first started gleaning in Boaz's field. Naomi also is insecure about where she and Ruth will live and on what they will survive in the coming months. She is convinced that she must take action, and she believes that it is God's will that she send Ruth to Boaz.

———

QUESTION: Many commentators wonder how Naomi could have asked Ruth to commit an immoral act—to seduce Boaz. How do these commentators explain Naomi's actions?

ANSWER: One explanation is that Naomi showed compassion for Boaz and Ruth, both of whom had lost their families, by bringing them together.[13] Another explanation is that of *hora'at sha'ah*—"exceptional measures."[14] Naomi felt that time was running out and that she had to take immediate action to bring Ruth and Boaz together; as the expression goes, "God helps those who help themselves." A third explanation is that Naomi was guided by *ru'ach ha-kodesh*—"the Holy Spirit" or prophetic inspiration.[15] Some say that people who have suffered greatly are closer to God than other people; because of the tragedies Naomi had experienced—the loss of her husband and sons—Naomi was divinely inspired and knew that the descendents of Boaz and Ruth would be destined for greatness.

Time and again the Tanakh teaches that God works in mysterious ways: the inappropriate sexual relationship between Lot and his older daughter produced Moab, from whom Ruth was descended; just as the relationship between Judah and Tamar (father-in-law and daughter-in-law) produced Perez, from whom Boaz was descended; and the relationship between David and Bathsheba (whose union came about when David saw the already married Bathsheba bathing on a nearby rooftop) produced King Solomon.

———

QUESTION: How did Naomi suggest that Ruth discreetly arrange to be with Boaz?

ANSWER: Naomi knew that Boaz was watching over his harvest at night to guard against thieves. Naomi instructed Ruth to stealthily make her way to the threshing floor, wait for Boaz to finish eating and drinking, and then wait for him to go to bed.

———

QUESTION: What was Ruth to do once Boaz lay down to sleep?

ANSWER: Once Boaz lay down, Ruth was to uncover his feet and lie down as well.

———

QUESTION: Why did Naomi tell Ruth to uncover Boaz's feet?

ANSWER: In order to redeem property, the redeemer removes his shoe and hands it to the other party to effect the transfer. Uncovering Boaz's feet, Naomi felt, would remind Boaz of his obligation to redeem Ruth. The redemption of property is discussed more fully in chapter 4.

QUESTION: Ruth agreed to go to Boaz in the middle of the night only out of respect for Naomi's wishes. Why was Ruth ambivalent about going?

ANSWER: Ruth was embarrassed to initiate contact with Boaz in hopes that he would marry her. She was concerned that Boaz would get frightened, become angry, or even lash out violently if he sensed somebody sneaking onto the threshing floor.

QUESTION: What did Naomi say to reassure Ruth that she was doing the right thing?

ANSWER: Naomi told Ruth not to worry, that Boaz would tell her what to do (3:4).

QUESTION: There are only two places in the *Book of Ruth* where a word is recited when the *megillah* is read aloud that is not found in the text, and in both cases it is the same word. What is that word?

ANSWER: *Elai*, which means "to me" (3:5; the second instance occurs in verse 17).

QUESTION: How do we surmise from the text that Ruth was reluctant to go to Boaz at night?

ANSWER: After listening to Naomi's directions to bathe, anoint herself, dress up, and go down to the threshing floor without letting Boaz see her, it is written (*ketiv*) that Ruth replied to Naomi: "I will do everything you say" (3:5). However, when the text is read aloud in the synagogue (*keri*), the word *elai* is added: "I will do everything you tell [*me*]."

According to the Sages, the absence of the word *elai* in the text suggests that Ruth felt uncomfortable with the instructions Naomi gave *to her* because they were not in keeping with Ruth's sense of modesty and dignity. The addition of the word *elai* in the reading, however, demonstrates that Ruth was willing to comply with Naomi's wishes. Other commentators suggest that the absence of the word *elai* in the text but its inclusion in the reading demonstrates that Ruth knew that the outcome of the meeting with Boaz did not rest in *her* hands, or even in Naomi's hands, but in God's hands.[16]

QUESTION: Verse 6 states that Ruth "went down to the threshing floor and did just as her mother-in-law had instructed her." Did Ruth follow Naomi's instructions to the letter?

ANSWER: No. Verse 7 says "Boaz ate and drank, and in a cheerful mood went to lie down beside the grainpile." The verse continues, "Then [Ruth] went over stealthily and uncovered his feet and lay down." But it mentions nothing about her having anointed herself or put on her finery.

———

QUESTION: Why didn't Ruth anoint herself or dress in her best clothes?

ANSWER: Ruth did not want to attract attention to herself. She was embarrassed about sneaking onto the threshing floor and did not want the other workers to see her. She also wanted to surprise Boaz. Therefore, the Sages say, she did not anoint herself or put on her good clothing until she reached the threshing floor.

———

QUESTION: What biblical passage does verse 7 of the *Book of Ruth*, which says, "Boaz ate and drank" and was in a "cheerful mood," recall?

ANSWER: *Deuteronomy* 8:10 teaches: "When you have eaten your fill, give thanks to the Lord your God for the good land that He has given you." Some commentators say that during the famine, while food was scarce, Boaz deliberately limited his consumption of food in order to share in the communal suffering. According to the Aramaic Targum, Boaz thanked God for having accepted his prayers and ended the famine, for he was now able to eat a satisfying meal.[17]

———

QUESTION: Where else do we find the words quoted above from *Deuteronomy* 8:10?

ANSWER: We recite them in the third paragraph of the Grace after Meals.

———

QUESTION: Why does verse 7 say that Boaz "went to lie down beside the grainpile"?

ANSWER: From this spot Boaz could watch all that was going on.

———

QUESTION: It is fascinating to compare the wording in *Genesis* 19:30 to that of *Ruth* 3:7. In what way are the texts similar and in what way do they differ from each other?

ANSWER: After the destruction of Sodom and Gomorrah, and after Lot's wife had been turned into a pillar of salt because she disobeyed God's command and looked back at the ruined cities, Lot and his two daughters hid in a *me'arah*—"cave." Believing that they were the only people left on earth, Lot's daughters got their father drunk and had intimate relations with him, "that we may maintain life through our father" (*Genesis* 19:32).

Ruth 3:7 tells us that "Boaz ate and drank . . ." and then "went to lie down beside the *aremah*"—"grainpile."

The similarities of the words *me'arah* and *aremah* lead us to connect the two stories, but what different outcomes they produced! Lot drank on an empty stomach and was so inebriated he did not even know that he had engaged in intimate relations with his daughters. Boaz, on the other hand, having survived a terrible famine, was grateful to God for all that he had had to eat and drink. Later, when Boaz awoke and found Ruth lying at his feet, he would not engage in inappropriate intimate relations as Lot had with his daughters, but would reassure Ruth that in the morning he would take care of the entire matter.

The Moabites, from whom Ruth was descended, were themselves the products of the sinful union between Lot and his older daughter. Engaged together in *tikkun olam,* Ruth and Boaz "repaired" the sins of the wicked Lot.[18]

———

QUESTION: Boaz was a righteous man and the head judge of the high court of Israel. By sending Ruth down to the threshing floor to lie at his feet, wasn't Naomi deliberately placing temptation in front of him?

ANSWER: Had Naomi approached Boaz directly, he would have told her that Ruth would be happier as the wife of a relative more closely related to Elimelech than he. But Naomi was convinced that Boaz was meant to redeem Ruth. She knew that he would not succumb to temptation (indeed, his name means "strength"), but would instead be deeply moved by Ruth's actions and realize that they were solely for the purpose of heaven.

———

QUESTION: When did Boaz discover Ruth?

ANSWER: Something startled Boaz in the middle of the night. When he looked around, he realized that a woman—Ruth—was lying at his feet (3:8).

———

QUESTION: Were there any risks involved in Ruth going to Boaz in the middle of the night?

ANSWER: Surprised to find Ruth lying at his feet, Boaz might have castigated her. Instead, he would bless her. King David, Ruth and Boaz's great-grandson, wrote in the book of *Psalms* (119:62), "I wake at midnight to express my gratitude to You [God] for your righteous words." This verse refers not only to the great praises sung by David to God but alludes to Ruth's visit to Boaz in the middle of the night. Had not the union of Ruth and Boaz been blessed by God, there would have been no King David.

———

QUESTION: Is there anything else significant about the midnight hour?

ANSWER: The Tanakh recounts numerous miracles that took place at midnight, a time of transformation and risk-taking:

At midnight Abraham defeated the four kings who had taken his nephew, Lot, captive (*Genesis* 14:15).

God appeared in a midnight dream to Abimelech, king of Gerar, telling him that he would die because he had taken Sarah, Abraham's wife, to his palace (*Genesis* 20:3).

God appeared in a midnight dream to Laban to warn him not to harm Jacob (*Genesis* 31:24).

Jacob wrestled with the angel in the middle of the night (*Genesis* 32:25).

The tenth plague—the killing of all firstborn Egyptian sons—occurred at midnight; it was this plague that finally convinced Pharaoh to free the Israelites from bondage (*Exodus* 12:29).

The prophet Deborah recounted how Yael killed Sisera, the Canaanite commander of King Jabin's army, at midnight (*Judges* 5:20).

In a war between Judah and Assyria, an angel of God entered the Assyrian camp at night, killing thousands of soldiers and sending King Sennacherib of Assyria fleeing in defeat (*2 Kings* 19:35–36).

In the *Book of Esther,* King Ahasuerus, unable to sleep at night, had his book of chronicles read to him and was reminded of the fact that Mordecai had saved his life (*Esther* 6:1–2).

Belshazzar, son (or, more likely, grandson) of Nebuchadnezzar, threw a party to which he invited all the noblemen of his kingdom to drink from the gold and silver vessels his father (or grandfather) had ransacked from the Temple. Suddenly, the fingers of a human hand appeared and wrote a mysterious message on the wall. Only the prophet Daniel could interpret that message—

which warned that Belshazzar's days were numbered. That very night, Belshazzar was killed (*Daniel* 5).

———

QUESTION: What does the word *va-yilafet* mean?

ANSWER: The word *va-yilafet* means to "turn around" or "pull back." Startled to find somebody lying at his feet, Boaz might have thought it was a ghost or a demon and pulled quickly away. Upon realizing that it was a woman lying at his feet, Boaz also might have become physically aroused. Yet he was able to control his desires and behavior. Rashi compares Boaz's ability to overcome temptation to that of Joseph, who worked in the home of Potiphar, Pharaoh's chief steward, and who refused the flagrant advances of Potiphar's wife (*Genesis* 39).[19]

———

QUESTION: What did Boaz do after he pulled back?

ANSWER: Boaz had slept on the threshing floor of his barn to prevent thieves from stealing his harvest. When he realized it was not a thief threatening him but a woman lying at his feet, he calmed down. His fear may have been replaced by embarrassment: as a highly devout individual, he surely was concerned about the propriety of the situation.

———

QUESTION: What did Boaz do next?

ANSWER: According to the Midrash, Boaz immediately washed his hands.[20] Because it is forbidden to mention God's name in worship or to utter words of Torah before ritually washing one's hands upon arising from sleep, observant Jews wash their hands even before getting out of bed. After dressing and rinsing their mouths (except on public fast days), they wash again and recite the morning blessings.

QUESTION: What were Boaz's first words to Ruth after discovering her lying at his feet?

ANSWER: Boaz asked Ruth, "Who are you?" (3:9).

QUESTION: What did Ruth reply?

ANSWER: She answered: "I am your handmaid Ruth. Spread your robe over your handmaid, for you are a redeeming kinsman" (3:9).

QUESTION: What does the phrase "spread your robe over your handmaid" mean?

ANSWER: This was a formulaic phrase for betrothal. In other words, Ruth was asking Boaz to fulfill the duties of the redeeming kinsman by marrying her, thus insuring that Mahlon's name would live on and his property remain in the family.

———

QUESTION: The word in verse 9 meaning "your robe"—*khenafekha*—has another meaning. What is it?

ANSWER: The word *khenafekha* also means "your wings": "Spread your wings over your handmaid."

———

QUESTION: What is the significance of this definition?

ANSWER: Birds shelter each other in their wings when they mate. The phrase can be understood as a plea for protection. Ruth did not want to sell Elimelech's property to a stranger; she wanted it to remain in the family. She also wanted to ensure that the name of her deceased husband, Mahlon, would be perpetuated. This was the "protection" that Ruth sought and that could be achieved if Boaz agreed to marry her.

———

QUESTION: What did Boaz mean in verse 10 when he said to Ruth, "Your latest deed of loyalty is greater than the first..."

ANSWER: Boaz felt that greater than Ruth's deeds of burying her husband and leaving her family and friends to accompany her mother-in-law to Bethlehem was her willingness to marry an elderly man in order to carry on her husband's name. Boaz continues in verse 10: "... you have not turned to younger men, whether poor or rich."

This is yet another example of Ruth setting aside her personal desires—for a husband her own age—in order to secure the family name and property.[21]

QUESTION: From a simple reading of verse 11, it seems that Boaz was willing to do whatever Ruth wanted. What did Boaz say?

ANSWER: "And now, daughter, have no fear. I will do in your behalf whatever you ask, for all the elders of my town know what a fine woman you are."

QUESTION: Does this mean that Boaz immediately agreed to marry Ruth?

ANSWER: No. As we learn from verse 12, Boaz knew there was another redeeming kinsman more closely related to Naomi and Ruth than he.

QUESTION: How was the other redeemer related to Naomi?

ANSWER: Boaz was Elimelech's nephew, while the other redeemer was Elimelech's brother, making the other redeemer more closely related to Naomi than Boaz.[22]

QUESTION: Do we know the name of the other redeemer?

ANSWER: In verse 13, Boaz says to Ruth, "Stay for the night. Then in the morning, if [the other] will act as a redeemer, good! let him redeem..." Some Sages say the Hebrew word *tov*, translated above as "good," actually refers to the name of the other redeemer. In other words, "If Tov wishes to redeem you, let him do so..." Other commentators disagree. They believe that if the redeemer's name was Tov, then Boaz would have referred to him by name in chapter 4, verse 1, instead of as *peloni almoni*, which means "so-and-so."[23]

———

QUESTION: Why did Boaz tell Ruth to "Stay for the night" (3:13)?

ANSWER: Boaz told Ruth to sleep in the granary rather than return home, because it would have been dangerous for Ruth to be out walking alone in the middle of the night. Her safety was Boaz's primary concern, even if it put them in a compromising position.

———

QUESTION: Although Boaz did not promise to marry Ruth in verse 12, he indicated that he would marry Ruth if the other redeemer did not wish to do so (3:13). To seal his vow, he uttered the unusual expression *Chai Hashem*, "as the Lord lives!" What did this expression signal?

ANSWER: After Boaz mentioned the other redeemer, Ruth may have thought to herself, "Is Boaz saying all these nice things simply to placate me? To flatter me? Would he rather that I marry the other redeemer?" Boaz's use of the expression "as the Lord lives!" demonstrated his clear commitment to Ruth and the seriousness of his intention to marry her.

QUESTION: What else does the expression "as the Lord lives!" indicate?

ANSWER: According to some commentators, Boaz was addressing himself to God rather than to Ruth. His *yetzer ha-ra*—"evil inclination"—was urging him to give in to temptation and engage in intimate relations with Ruth. Boaz prayed to God for the strength to withstand those impulses.[24]

QUESTION: Does the expression "as the Lord lives!" appear elsewhere in the Tanakh? Where?

ANSWER: David used this same expression when he resisted the temptation to kill King Saul, swearing that, "...as the Lord lives, God Himself will strike [Saul] down, or his time will come and he will die, or he will go down to battle and perish. But God forbid that I should lay a hand on His anointed..." (*1 Samuel* 26:10–11).

QUESTION: Verse 14 tells us that that "[Ruth] lay at [Boaz's] feet until dawn. She rose before one person could distinguish another, for [Boaz] thought: 'Let it not be known that the woman came to the threshing floor.'" What is the meaning of this verse?

ANSWER: Ruth and Boaz awoke early so that no one would suspect that Ruth had been there. Boaz not only was concerned about his own reputation—he was known as an extremely righteous man, and an old one— but about Ruth's reputation. This is the meaning of the phrase, "Let it not be known that the woman came to the threshing floor."

———

QUESTION: What is the meaning of the word *beterem*, "before," in the phrase, "before one person could distinguish another"?

ANSWER: The Hebrew word *beterem* is spelled *beit-teit-reish-vav-mem*. The *vav*, whose numerical value is six, is superfluous. According to the Sages, the presence of the *vav* in the word indicates that Ruth spent six hours on the threshing floor with Boaz, a prolonged period of time, and yet nothing untoward occurred.[25]

———

QUESTION: When Boaz and Ruth awoke early in the morning, how did Boaz say goodbye to her?

ANSWER: Boaz asked Ruth to hold out the shawl she was wearing so that he could put in it a symbolic gift (3:15).

———

QUESTION: What kind of gift did Boaz give Ruth?

ANSWER: He gave Ruth six measures of barley.

———

QUESTION: How much is six measures equivalent to?

ANSWER: The text literally says that Boaz gave Ruth six grains of barley. Boaz was said to have been a very generous man, so it is puzzling that he would give her only six grains of barley. Nor does it make sense that he would give her six *se'ahs*—"standard measures"—of grain, for that would have been too much for her to carry home. Some Sages say that Boaz gave Ruth six symbolic grains of barley and then a larger quantity that she could take with her. Others suggest that the word *shesh* does not mean "six" but instead refers to a sixth of a *se'ah*, which would have been enough to feed herself and Naomi.[26]

———

QUESTION: Are there any other interpretations?

ANSWER: Yes. The Sages also interpret "six grains of barley" symbolically. Each grain represents one of six outstanding descendents of Ruth and Boaz: King David and the Messiah, of course; Daniel, prophet of the Babylonian exile; and Daniel's three companions in the court of Nebuchadnezzar—Hananiah, Mishael, and Azariah—who refused to renounce their Judaism even when they were thrown into a fiery furnace.[27]

———

QUESTION: It also is said that the six grains of barley represent the six attributes with which, according to the Scriptures, David was endowed. What are those attributes?

ANSWER: The *Book of Samuel* (*1 Samuel* 16:18) describes David as a musician, a man of valor, a prophet, an expressive speaker, handsome, and always imbued with the spirit of God.

———

QUESTION: Some say that Boaz placed the barley on Ruth's back. Others interpret the words of this verse differently. Where do they say that Boaz placed the barley?

ANSWER: They say Boaz probably placed the grain on Ruth's head, which is how women carried great weights in those days and still do in many Middle Eastern and African countries.

———

QUESTION: When Ruth returned to Naomi in the morning, Naomi asked her, "How is it with you, daughter?"—literally, "Who are you, my daughter?" (3:16). Did Naomi not recognize her own daughter-in-law?

ANSWER: Of course Naomi recognized Ruth! What she really wanted to know was what had transpired between Ruth and Boaz the night before: had Boaz agreed to marry Ruth? Had they already consummated their relationship? By referring to Ruth as her daughter, Naomi sought to reassure Ruth of her affection for her.

———

QUESTION: How did Ruth reply to her mother-in-law's question?

ANSWER: Ruth told Naomi "all that the man had done for her" (3:16). Ruth trusted Naomi unconditionally and confided in her all the details of what had taken place the night before.

———

QUESTION: Ruth also showed Naomi something. What was it?

ANSWER: Ruth showed Naomi the six measures of barley that Boaz had given her.

———

QUESTION: What did Ruth say to Naomi when she showed her the barley?

ANSWER: Ruth said, "He gave me these six measures of barley, saying [to me], 'Do not go back to your mother-in-law empty-handed'" (3:17).

———

QUESTION: Just as the word *elai* ("to me") is added in verse 5 of chapter 3 when the *Book of Ruth* is read aloud in the synagogue, so, too, is the word *elai* added in this verse, 17, when the *Book of Ruth* is read aloud. Why?

ANSWER: When Boaz gave Ruth the six measures of barley, he did not mention that they were for Naomi. But Ruth knew that it would be of great comfort to Naomi to feel that Boaz was looking out not just for Ruth, but for her as well. That is why the word *elai* is added before the quotation, "Do not go back to your mother-in-law empty-handed."[28]

———

QUESTION: Is there another explanation?

ANSWER: Ruth did not want Naomi to think that the barley represented a payment for Ruth's nighttime visit to Boaz or a farewell gift.

———

QUESTION: Is there yet another explanation for the omission of the word *elai* in the text?

ANSWER: Yes. According to some commentators, the omission of the word *elai* in the *ketiv* indicates that

Boaz, always modest, did not look directly at Ruth when he spoke to her during their conversation the night before.[29]

———

QUESTION: Naomi surely sensed Ruth's anxiety about her fate: would Boaz marry her? Would the other redeemer want to marry her? What did Naomi advise Ruth to do in the last verse of chapter 3?

ANSWER: Naomi said to Ruth, "Stay here, daughter, till you learn how the matter turns out. For [Boaz] will not rest, but will settle the matter today" (3:18).

———

QUESTION: Naomi's words were intended to assuage Ruth's concerns. How so?

ANSWER: Naomi knew that Boaz was a man of his word, and that if he made a commitment to Ruth, he would honor it.[30] Naomi also knew that Boaz was a man of action. He would not put off his talk with the other redeemer but intended to reach a resolution that very day. Therefore, Naomi hoped that Ruth would think positively and remain calm.

———

QUESTION: What did Naomi mean when she said "how the matter turns out"?

ANSWER: Once again we are taught that everything

is in the hands of God. Ruth approached Boaz and indicated her willingness to marry him. Now she had to wait patiently for God to decide her future.[31]

Chapter 4

Synopsis

Boaz meets the other potential redeemer— *peloni almoni*—at the gates of the city. Although *peloni almoni* expresses interest in buying Elimelech's land, he declines to marry Ruth. Therefore, Boaz, with the elders of the city as his witnesses, fulfills his promise to marry Ruth and redeem all of Elimelech, Mahlon, and Chilion's property. Ruth and Boaz immediately conceive a child, and Ruth gives birth to a son, Obed, father of Jesse, father of King David.

———

QUESTION: Verse 1 of chapter 4 tells us that "Boaz had gone to the gate and sat down there." What do we learn from this sentence?

ANSWER: Boaz, like his grandfather Nahshon (the first person to walk into the Red Sea as God miraculously split its waters during the Exodus from Egypt[1]) and his great-grandson David, was a man of action. As soon as morning broke, Boaz set out for the gate of the city to fulfill the promise that he had made to Ruth: to find the other redeemer and settle, once and for all, which one of the two of them would redeem Naomi's daughter-in-law.

QUESTION: Why did Boaz feel duty-bound to take immediate action?

ANSWER: The fact that Ruth had come to him in the middle of the night and lay down at his feet was an indication of the desperate straits in which she and Naomi found themselves. It was incumbent upon Boaz, a God-fearing man, a community leader, and a judge, to concur with his fellow judges to resolve Ruth's future.

QUESTION: What lesson do we learn from Boaz's behavior?

ANSWER: We learn that a person must put forward his or her best efforts. The outcome, however, is in the hands of the Almighty.

QUESTION: What was significant about the gate of the city?

ANSWER: Bethlehem was an important city; this we know because the city had a gate, meaning it was walled and fortified. All important business was conducted at the city gate; it was the site of the marketplace and the court.

Boaz was said to have been a judge—some say the chief judge of Bethlehem[2]—so it was natural for him to sit at the city gate. There, Boaz knew that he would find the elders of the city and that they would witness his meeting with *peloni almoni* (and later his marriage to Ruth).

——

QUESTION: Is there another interpretation?

ANSWER: Some commentators say that Boaz not only sat at the gate of the city to await the other redeemer but actually convened a special meeting with the other judges of Bethlehem in order to settle Ruth's fate.[3]

——

QUESTION: Where else does the Torah refer to the "gate" of the city?

ANSWER: *Deuteronomy* 25:5–10 details the *chalitzah* procedure—the steps that a childless woman must follow if her deceased husband's brother does not wish to marry her (discussed in further detail below). Verse 7 says that first she is to go to the gate [of the city], to the elders. There are many other references in the Tanakh to the gates of the city, including *Genesis* 19:1 and 34:20, *Deuteronomy* 16:18 and 21:19, and *Proverbs* 31:23 and 31:31.[4]

——

QUESTION: When faced with a difficult situation, a true leader rises to the occasion. The final outcome, however, is in God's hands. A miracle occurred as soon as Boaz and his fellow judges sat together to discuss Ruth's future. What was it?

ANSWER: Out of the blue, the other redeemer—*peloni almoni*—walked by.

QUESTION: Was *peloni almoni* aware that Naomi and Ruth had returned from Moab several months before?

ANSWER: Some commentators believe that he was aware of Naomi and Ruth's presence in Bethlehem; others do not believe that he was aware.

QUESTION: Was *peloni almoni* aware that he was the closest redeemer?

ANSWER: Again, some believe that he was ignorant of the fact that he was the closest redeemer, while others believe that he intentionally ignored Naomi and Ruth.

QUESTION: As we discussed in chapter 3, some say that *peloni almoni's* name was Tov, a Hebrew word meaning "good" (3:13); in chapter 4, verse 1, he is referred to simply as *peloni almoni*, the equivalent of "so-and-so." If his name was Tov, why is he called *peloni almoni* here?

ANSWER: As the closest relative to Elimelech and his sons, *peloni almoni* had the obligation to redeem Ruth.

But he had not stepped forward to do so. Therefore, he was not even referred to by name, a lesson for all those who do not come forward to do the right thing. Others, however, say that the prophet Samuel, who wrote the *Book of Ruth*, did not want to shame the redeemer and so did not refer to him by name.

——

QUESTION: What is the meaning of the phrase *peloni almoni*?

ANSWER: *Peloni almoni* means "anonymous."

——

QUESTION: How does Rashi define the word *almoni*?

ANSWER: According to Rashi, *almoni* means "widowhood." *Peloni almoni*, says Rashi, was "widowed" from Jewish law. He should have known the recently adjudicated law that Moabite women could convert to Judaism (although Moabite men were prohibited from doing so) but apparently was unfamiliar with it. The word *almoni* also may be related to the word *alam*, "to be struck dumb" or "mute." *Peloni almoni* kept silent and did not come forward to inquire about Ruth and Naomi's well-being or offer to help them in any way. Perhaps *peloni almoni* is derived from the word *pele*, which means "hidden" or "covered": Rabbi Me'ir Leibush Malbim says that it is impossible to know why *peloni almoni* rejected the mitzvah of redeeming Ruth.

——

QUESTION: The Sages say it was a miracle that *peloni almoni* walked by the gate as Boaz was meeting with his fellow judges to discuss Naomi and Ruth's situation. Others say that *peloni almoni* had been summoned to a meeting. If so, why didn't Boaz refer to him by his real name?

ANSWER: *Peloni almoni* had successfully ignored Naomi and Ruth to this point. He clearly was unhappy about being summoned to appear before the elders of Bethlehem. Boaz, therefore, derisively referred to him as *peloni almoni*. [5]

———

QUESTION: A name is said to express an individual's personality. With an appellation like Tov, how could this man fail to act in a kind manner?

ANSWER: While we believe that a person's name is a reflection of his or her character, God gives us freedom of choice. *Peloni almoni* chose to distance himself from family concerns and problems.

———

QUESTION: The last sentence of verse 1 reads, "[Boaz] called, 'Come over and sit down here, so-and-so!' And [*peloni almoni*] came over and sat down." Why is it necessary to say that *peloni almoni* came over and sat down?

ANSWER: *Peloni almoni* was Boaz's uncle, yet he deferred to Boaz, waiting for Boaz's instructions to sit and then waiting while Boaz assembled the other elders of the city.

———

QUESTION: Verse 2 tells us that Boaz "took ten elders of the town and said, 'Be seated here'; and they sat down." Why did Boaz gather a quorum of men?

ANSWER: Boaz gathered ten men to witness the events that were about to occur: *peloni almoni's* decision about redeeming the property that Naomi was offering for sale and the marriage of Ruth to a redeemer, either *peloni almoni* or Boaz.

———

QUESTION: Why did the ten elders wait to be seated until instructed to do so by Boaz?

ANSWER: Like *peloni almoni*, the elders of the city deferred to Boaz, head of the court, and waited until he was seated before sitting down.

———

QUESTION: What is the significance of the number ten?

ANSWER: We learn from the *Book of Ruth* that the presence of a quorum is required for the recitation of the marital benedictions. Additionally, the presence of ten elders was required here to publicly confirm the law allowing a Moabite woman to enter into the community of Israel as a convert.[6]

———

QUESTION: As a judge and one of the leaders of his generation, why did Boaz gather ten men rather than nine, counting himself as the tenth?

ANSWER: Boaz had a personal stake in the outcome of their decision. He recused himself, further testament to his righteousness.

———

QUESTION: After Boaz convened the quorum of ten elders, he turned to *peloni almoni* and said, "Naomi, now returned from the country of Moab, must sell the piece of land which belonged to our kinsman Elimelech" (4:3). In verse 4, Boaz continued, "I thought I should disclose the matter to you and say: Acquire it in the presence of those seated here and in the presence of the elders of my people. If you are willing to redeem it, redeem! But if you will not redeem, tell me, that I may know. For there is no one to redeem but you, and I come after you." Why did Boaz use the words *keneh* ("acquire" or "buy") and *ge'al* ("redeem")?

ANSWER: Boaz wanted to make sure that *peloni almoni* understood that this was a two-part transaction, involving both the sale of property and the redemption of Ruth. He believed that *peloni almoni* would agree to purchase the property that belonged to Naomi; however, he was not sure that *peloni almoni* would agree to marry Ruth.[7]

Another important distinction should be drawn between the words *keneh* and *ge'al*: one who makes a purchase is looking for the best possible price; one who redeems does so to help a member of the family and might even be willing to pay more than the asking price.

———

QUESTION: Although we translate the phrase *makhrah Naomi* as "Naomi...must sell...," the word *makhrah* is in the past tense. Had Naomi already sold the property? Would she have been permitted to do so?

ANSWER: Naomi had not already sold the property. What she had done was put the matter into the hands of the court—of which Boaz was head. If the property did not remain in the family, it would have to be sold to an outsider.

———

QUESTION: How did *peloni almoni* respond to Boaz?

ANSWER: *Peloni almoni* quickly responded that he would redeem the property of Elimelech.

———

QUESTION: As soon as *peloni almoni* agreed to redeem Naomi's property, Boaz informed him of the condition attached to the transaction. What did Boaz say?

ANSWER: Boaz stipulated, "When you acquire the property from Naomi and from Ruth the Moabite, you must also acquire the wife of the deceased, so as to perpetuate the name of the deceased upon his estate" (4:5).

———

QUESTION: Did *peloni almoni* agree to this condition?

ANSWER: No! *Peloni almoni* quickly responded, "Then I cannot redeem it for myself, lest I impair my own estate" (4:6).

———

QUESTION: Why did *peloni almoni* refuse to marry such a beautiful woman as Ruth? Was he concerned about money—the costs of supporting a new wife—or other matters?

ANSWER: *Peloni almoni* may have been eager to consummate the deal when it involved property, but he could not envision the prospect of a new bride.

———

QUESTION: Is there another reason why *peloni almoni* refused to marry Ruth?

ANSWER: Polygamy clearly was accepted in the ancient Jewish world. According to some Sages, *peloni almoni* was already married and had children.[8] He may have been afraid of hurting or angering his wife, or creating friction among his children. Other Sages say that *peloni almoni* believed that Mahlon and Chilion had died as punishment for marrying Moabite women; he feared he would suffer the same fate.[9]

——

QUESTION: Why else may *peloni almoni* have been reluctant to marry Ruth?

ANSWER: According to Rashi, *peloni almoni* believed that Jewish men were forbidden to marry Moabite women, even those who had converted to Judaism, as had Ruth. Though he did not fear for himself, he was concerned about any children he and Ruth might have—that they would be disqualified from receiving an inheritance and be treated as outcasts in the community.

——

QUESTION: When did the Jewish approach to polygamy change?

ANSWER: The tenth-century Ashkenazi legal authority, Gershom ben Yehudah, known as Rabbenu Gershom, is credited with the prohibition against polygamy. The practice of husbands having more than one wife could lead to terrible marital discord (in the Torah we have the examples of Abraham and his wives Sarah and Hagar, and Jacob and his wives Rachel and Leah) or licentiousness. Rabbenu Gershom's goal was to simplify and harmonize family life, as well as to ease the plight of Jews in a Christian society that prohibited polygamy. Among Sephardi Jews, polygamy was an accepted practice until the middle of the twentieth century.

———

QUESTION: Verse 7 outlines a longstanding procedure in Israel for the redemption of property. What was the procedure?

ANSWER: The redeemer would remove his shoe and hand it to the person from whom he was redeeming the property; this sealed the legal transfer of property. So, Boaz removed his shoe and handed it to *peloni almoni*.

———

QUESTION: Sometimes readers mistakenly confuse the transfer or acquisition of property (in Hebrew, *kinyan*) described in the *Book of Ruth* with *chalitzah*. What is the *chalitzah* ceremony?

ANSWER: The Biblical law of levirate marriage (*Deuteronomy* 25:5–10), in Hebrew *yibbum*, requires that a man marry his childless brother's widow in order to perpetuate his deceased brother's name. If the man refuses to marry his sister-in-law, the *chalitzah* ceremony, as discussed in chapter 2, is performed: the widow takes a shoe (worn specially for the occasion and called a *chalitzah* shoe[10]) from her brother-in-law's foot and spits on the ground in front of him, a public display of the contempt in which she holds him for his refusal to marry her and have children. This ceremony is rarely performed today.

———

QUESTION: Why did Boaz hand his shoe to *peloni almoni* and not to Naomi or Ruth, since Elimelech's property belonged to them?

ANSWER: Rather than the actual transfer of property, what is being described here is the *right* to transfer property, which *peloni almoni* is relinquishing in favor of Boaz.

———

QUESTION: What did Boaz do next?

ANSWER: Boaz proclaimed to all the people gathered at the city gate: "You are witnesses today that I am acquiring from Naomi all that belonged to Elimelech and all that belonged to Chilion and Mahlon" (4:9). By fulfilling the mitzvah of redemption in the presence of the elders of the city, he restored Naomi and Ruth's honor before the townspeople of Bethlehem.

———

QUESTION: This was not all that Boaz said before the many people gathered there. What else did he declare?

ANSWER: "I am also acquiring Ruth the Moabite, the wife of Mahlon, as my wife, so as to perpetuate the name of the deceased upon his estate, that the name of the deceased may not disappear from among his kinsmen and from the gate of his home town. You are witnesses today" (4:10).

QUESTION: Why did Boaz declare twice, once in verse 9 and again in verse 10, "You are witnesses today"?

ANSWER: According to the Malbim, Boaz gathered two groups of witnesses, the first to witness his purchase of the land, and the second to witness his marriage to Ruth.[11]

QUESTION: Was Boaz taking a chance in marrying Ruth?

ANSWER: Many would say that marrying Ruth was a risky thing to do: her first husband had died, *peloni almoni* was afraid to marry her, and her Moabite origins could present political difficulties for a new husband. Boaz's willingness to marry Ruth exemplified his faith and strength.

QUESTION: What precedent did Boaz set by marrying Ruth?

ANSWER: The marriage of Boaz to Ruth, a Moabite convert to Judaism, was the first sanctioned by the leaders of the Jewish people. The fact that Boaz and Ruth's marriage took place before so many witnesses removed any doubts about its validity or legitimacy—though the issue arose again when David became king.

———

QUESTION: Usually Naomi's sons are referred to as Mahlon and Chilion, in that order. Why does Boaz reverse the order in verse 9?

ANSWER: Boaz reversed the order of their names to emphasize his legal claim over all of the property that had belonged to Elimelech, Chilion, and Mahlon—lest Orpah or any of her descendents bring claim for a share of Chilion's estate.[12]

———

QUESTION: Boaz uses the same word *kaniti*—"I am acquiring"—to refer to Naomi's property (4:9) and to Ruth (4:10). Does he value his wife no more than he values land?

ANSWER: The Hebrew word *kanah*—"to acquire"— is used for the action of taking a wife, as well as acquiring property. In Jewish law the wife is regarded as a beloved and honored partner in the sacred task of building a home and raising a family. Boaz had tremendous respect for Ruth and certainly did not consider her his property.

That is why he mentioned the acquisition of Naomi's property apart from taking Ruth to be his wife.

———

QUESTION: How did the many people gathered at the gate to the city respond to Boaz's proclamation about marrying Ruth?

ANSWER: The townspeople offered Boaz three blessings—a strong marriage, a prosperous future, and that, despite his age, he would merit children: "We are [witnesses]. May the Lord make the woman who is coming into your house like [the matriarchs] Rachel and Leah, both of whom built up the House of Israel! Prosper in Ephrathah and perpetuate your name in Bethlehem. And may your house be like the house of Perez whom Tamar bore to Judah—through the offspring which the Lord will give you by this young woman [Ruth]" (4:11–12).[13]

———

QUESTION: Why did the witnesses ask God to make Ruth like Rachel and Leah rather than like the matriarchs Sarah and Rebekah?

ANSWER: Rachel and Leah were the daughters of a wicked, idol-worshipping father, just as Ruth was the product of a wicked, idolatrous nation. Yet the righteous Rachel and Leah, devoted sisters, left their home, just as Ruth had done, and merited a righteous husband and offspring. The people of Bethlehem wished the same for Ruth.[14]

———

QUESTION: Is there another reason the townspeople wished Boaz a wife like Rachel and Leah rather than like Sarah and Rebekah?

ANSWER: Sarah and Rebekah each had one good son—the patriarchs Isaac and Jacob—and one challenging son—Ishmael and Esau. The townspeople prayed that Boaz and Ruth's offspring would be only righteous.[15]

————

QUESTION: What is the meaning of the second blessing, "Prosper in Ephrathah and perpetuate your name in Bethlehem"?

ANSWER: The names Ephrathah—Ephrath—and Bethlehem are used interchangeably in the Tanakh to refer to the same city. Ephrath also is another name for the world to come. Boaz's marriage to Ruth was sanctioned not only by the people of Bethlehem but by the heavenly court.[16]

————

QUESTION: Who were Judah and Tamar, and what do we know about their son, Perez?

ANSWER: As we discussed in chapter 2, Tamar was married to Er, the oldest son of Judah, who was the fourth son of the patriarch Jacob. Er died, and because he did not have children, Judah married Tamar to his second oldest son, Onan. Onan produced no off-spring with Tamar to carry on Er's name, and Onan, too, died. Judah then promised Tamar that his youngest son, Shelah, would marry her when he grew up, so Tamar returned to her father's house to wait. Years went by, Shelah grew up, but Judah did not arrange for Shelah and Tamar to marry. When Tamar learned that Judah's wife had died and that Judah was coming to shear sheep in Timnah, she disguised herself as a harlot and waited for Judah at the entrance to the town of Enaim. Judah, not realizing that the harlot was Tamar, had intimate re-lations with her and left his seal, cord, and staff as a pledge until he could send her payment for her services. However, when he sent a servant to pay Tamar as prom-ised, the servant was unable to locate her.

A few months later, Judah was outraged to learn that Tamar was pregnant. As she was being taken out to be burned, she sent a message to her father-in-law, saying, "I am with child by the man to whom these [seal, cord, and staff] belong." When Judah recognized those ob-jects as his own, he said, "She is more in the right than I, inasmuch as I did not give her to my son Shelah" (*Genesis* 38:24–26).

Tamar would give birth to twins, Perez and Zerah. Boaz was a direct descendent of Perez.

QUESTION: Boaz married Ruth right away, and she conceived and bore a son. Why does verse 13 say, "The Lord let her conceive"?

ANSWER: Although Mahlon and Ruth were young when they married, they were unable to have children. God, however, so blessed the union of Boaz and Ruth that Ruth conceived right away.[17]

———

QUESTION: According to the Midrash[18], as soon as Ruth conceived, on the very first night of their marriage, Boaz died. Why did he not merit to see the birth of his son?

ANSWER: Even though, according to the Midrash, he was eighty years old, because Boaz married Ruth, he merited having a child. But once the child was conceived, the Sages explain, Boaz's soul had completed its mission, and Boaz died. Divine Providence directs the destiny of every human being.[19]

———

QUESTION: The last mention of Ruth's name occurs in verse 13. Why isn't her name mentioned after that?

ANSWER: After Ruth's marriage and the birth of her son, Obed, her mission also was complete and her place in Jewish history secure.[20]

———

QUESTION: Upon the birth of Ruth and Boaz's son, the women of Bethlehem blessed Naomi. What did they say to her?

ANSWER: "Blessed be the Lord, who has not withheld a redeemer from you today! May his name be perpetuated in Israel! He will renew your life and sustain your old age; for he is born of your daughter-in-law, who loves you and is better to you than seven sons" (4:14–15).

———

QUESTION: Verse 16 says, "Naomi took the child and held it to her bosom. She became its foster mother..." What does this mean?

ANSWER: Naomi was Ruth's role model; Ruth was confident that Naomi would raise the baby in the best possible way, teaching the child to live a proper Jewish life, as she had instructed Ruth. Ruth also knew that it would be therapeutic for Naomi—who had lost her own children, and seemingly the chance for grandchildren—to take care of the baby. According to one commentator,[21] Naomi literally was able to nurse the baby—proof that Mahlon's soul was reincarnated into Obed's body and reminiscent of the matriarch Sarah, who at ninety years of age gave birth to and nursed her son Isaac.[22]

———

QUESTION: Why did the neighbors say, "A son is born to Naomi!" (4:17), when it was Ruth who gave birth to the baby (4:13)?

ANSWER: The Sages say not only that Naomi raised

the baby, but that the baby was pure like Naomi and resembled Mahlon.[23]

***

QUESTION: Who named Ruth and Boaz's baby?

ANSWER: According to verse 17, "the women neighbors gave him a name, saying, 'A son is born to Naomi!'"

***

QUESTION: Why did Naomi's neighbors name the baby?

ANSWER: When Naomi returned to Bethlehem from Moab, she said to her neighbors, "Do not call me Naomi [which means 'pleasant'] . . . Call me Mara [which means 'bitter']" (1:20). Ruth's marriage to Boaz and the birth of Obed represented a complete reversal of fortune for Naomi and Ruth. Honor had been restored to Elimelech's family and continuity assured. The townspeople were no longer resentful of Naomi for having left Bethlehem with her husband and sons, but admired her and were eager to rejoice in her good fortune.

***

QUESTION: What did the women name the baby?

ANSWER: They named the baby Obed.

***

QUESTION: What is the meaning of the name Obed?

ANSWER: Obed means "servant of God." According to the Targum, Obed was granted the gift of prophecy and the promise that his descendents would be kings because he would serve (*oved*) God with a perfect heart, just as his mother and father had served God.

———

QUESTION: Verse 17 concludes with the names of Obed's son and grandson. Who were they?

ANSWER: Obed fathered a son named Jesse, and Jesse fathered David.

———

QUESTION: How does the *Book of Ruth* end?

ANSWER: The last verses of chapter 4, 18 through 22, list the descendents of Perez, son of Judah and Tamar: Hezron, Ram, Amminadab, Nahshon, Salmon, Boaz, Obed, Jesse, and David.

———

QUESTION: How many generations are included in this genealogy?

ANSWER: Beginning with Perez and ending with King David, this genealogy spans ten generations, an auspicious number in the Jewish tradition.[24]

———

QUESTION: Why is Boaz's father referred to as Salma in verse 20 and Salmon in verse 21?

ANSWER: The Sages say that the name change reflects the beginning of a new era: Boaz's father's generation was the first to enter the Holy Land after the Exodus from Egypt.

———

QUESTION: The Tanakh includes many genealogies. What is so special about the genealogy here?

ANSWER: In the Tanakh, genealogies are an important way of perpetuating the names of past generations. Through her marriage to Boaz, Ruth performed the mitzvah of perpetuating her husband's name for future generations. The last word of the *Book of Ruth* is "David," a man who became king not through bloodshed but as a reward by God for his loving-kindness and humility.

———

QUESTION: Though Naomi had lived through the death of her husband and sons and the degradation of her reputation in Bethlehem, by the end of the *Book of Ruth*, her reputation is restored, her life renewed (with the birth of Obed), and her family's legacy assured. How was Ruth rewarded?

ANSWER: For her great piety and kindness Ruth was rewarded with a secure future, her son Obed, and the promise that one of her descendents would be the "redeemer" of Israel (4:14) in a kingdom of "peace without end" (*Isaiah 9:6*).

———

QUESTION: What other reward did Ruth receive?

ANSWER: According to the Talmud, Ruth lived such a long life that she saw her great-great-grandson, Solomon, build the First Temple.

———

QUESTION: What final lessons do we learn from the *Book of Ruth*?

ANSWER: The *Book of Ruth* teaches many lessons. On one level, perhaps most significantly for its author, the prophet Samuel, the *Book of Ruth* is a political manifesto, designed to erase any doubts in the minds of ancient readers about King David's lineage and claim to the throne.

To modern readers, the lessons are more transcendent. Ruth and Naomi suffered great tragedies and setbacks in their lives, as did Boaz. Yet God had a plan for each of them, as He does for each of us. At the time that Ruth gave birth to Obed, she could not anticipate that one of her descendents would become the greatest king of Israel, King David, or that his son, Solomon, would build the First Temple, or that another of David's descendents would one day become the Messiah. But if the only thing we learn from the *Book of Ruth* is that life is fate and that everything is in God's hands, we are missing the greatest lesson of all: that it is up to each of us to make the world a better place, for ourselves and for others. And that the way we do this is through *tikkun olam*, becoming partners with God in repairing the world.[25]

The *Book of Genesis* teaches that after God created heaven and earth "and all their array," He "formed man from the dust of the earth. He blew into his nostrils the breath of life, and man became a living being" (*Genesis* 2:1–7). The dust represents man's earthly, physical nature; the breath of life that God blew into Adam's nostrils is, as the Zohar explains, God's own spirit, what we call the soul, in Hebrew *nefesh* or *neshamah*. These two aspects of man—the earthly and the heavenly, the physical and the spiritual, the touchable and the untouchable—are often in tension with each other.

In the opening verses of the *Book of Ruth*, we were introduced to Elimelech, husband of Naomi, and their two sons, Mahlon, and Chilion. A leader of the Jewish community in Bethlehem, Elimelech fled his home for the land of Moab when famine struck Israel. There, in Moab, Elimelech died, and ten years after his sons Mahlon and Chilion married Moabite women, they, too, died, leaving no heirs, nobody to carry on the family name. All three men are emblematic of the kind of person who puts his or her physical needs above all else; even *peloni almoni* was unwilling to extend a hand to Ruth if it meant risking his inheritance to his children.

Jewish literature is rife with examples of people just the opposite of Elimelech, Mahlon, Chilion, and *peloni almoni*—individuals for whom the spiritual life is all-encompassing. Ruth, Naomi, and Boaz, however, exemplify a third path that God has laid out for us: instead of our physical and spiritual natures waging war with each other, it is possible to live with them in balance.

Naomi did not return to Bethlehem until she was sure that the famine had ended and food was readily available. She encouraged her daughters-in-law to remain in Moab and return to their childhood homes, where all their needs would be met. Orpah, Chilion's wife, did, in the end, agree to remain in Moab, but Ruth, Mahlon's wife, refused to abandon Naomi and insisted on accompanying her to Bethlehem. It is difficult to imagine Naomi traveling back to Bethlehem by herself, but with Ruth's help, the two women reached Israel. Naomi depended on Ruth to provide for her needs; in turn, Naomi imbued Ruth with a love of Judaism and shared with her practical advice to attract Boaz's attention and win from him the promise of redemption.

Ruth knew that her mother-in-law needed somebody to accompany her on her return and to provide for her once they reached Bethlehem. That is why Ruth went to glean in Boaz's field. However, Ruth recognized a deeper hunger in herself, a longing for faith and holiness. That is why she converted to Judaism and continued to look to Naomi for spiritual and emotional guidance. When Ruth's son, Obed, was born, she counted on Naomi to help her raise him, knowing that his birth gave Naomi hope for the future.

Boaz, the Sages teach, buried his wife on the very day

that Naomi and Ruth returned to Bethlehem. Yet he continued his vigorous leadership of the Jewish people and continued to reach out to the poor, welcoming Ruth to glean in his fields and promising Ruth that he would redeem her, as he ultimately did.

All three—Ruth, Naomi, and Boaz—cared for and sustained each other. They were models of *tikkun olam* to the people of their day and continue to inspire Jews of every generation to repair the world. Furthermore, they insured that the names of those who had gone before them, Elimelech, Mahlon, and Chilion, would live on and that their souls finally would be at rest.

Just as God implants His spirit into a person when he or she is born, it is said that God draws His spirit out of an individual upon his or her death. Once the *neshamah*, the soul, has completed its mission on earth, it can return to God. The more good a person does on earth, the more deeply he or she will come to know God and the closer he or she will be to God in *olam ha-ba*—"the world to come."[26]

Notes

Abbreviations

J.T. = Jerusalem Talmud

M. = Mishnah

R. = Rabbi

T. = Babylonian Talmud

Introductory Questions

1. T. *Menachot* 89b; *Sifra* 12:4; T. *Kiddushin* 37a; Rashi, *Leviticus* 23:11.
2. T. *Beitzah* 5b; R. Yechi'el Michel Tuchachinsky, *Ir ha-Kodesh ve-ha-Mikdash* (Jerusalem: Makhon Yad, 1945).
3. R. Isaac Levy and R. Shlomo Asaf, *Challenge* (London: Encounter, 1970).
4. T. *Bava Batra* 14b.
5. J.T. *Chagigah* 2:1.
6. T. *Megillah* 14a.
7. *1 Samuel* 1–2.
8. *Ruth Rabbah* 1.
9. Zohar, *Balak* 104.
10. T. *Bava Batra* 91a; T. *Nazir* 23b.
11. *Me'am Lo'ez* (by R. Ya'akov Culi); T. *Nazir* 23b.
12. *Me'am Lo'ez*.

Chapter 1

1. T. *Megillah* 10b.
2. Ibn Ezra, *Ruth* 1.
3. *Ruth Rabbah* 1.
4. T. *Megillah* 14a.
5. T. *Bava Batra* 15b.
6. *Yalkut Shimoni, Ruth* 1:1.
7. *Etz Chayyim* (by R. Chayyim Vital, recording the words of R. Yitzchak Luria).
8. T. *Gittin* 11a.
9. *Me'am Lo'ez; Seder Olam Rabbah* (by R. Yosei ben Chalafta).
10. *Ruth Rabbah* 1.
11. *Shocher Tov.*
12. *Sifra.*
13. *Ruth Rabbah* 1.
14. Ibid.; T. *Bava Batra* 91b.
15. T. *Bava Batra* 81b.
16. T. *Bava Batra* 91b; see also *Zohar Chadash.*
17. T. *Sanhedrin* 22b; see also Rashi, *Ruth* 1:3.
18. *Ruth Rabbah* 1; *Zohar, Balak* 104; T. *Nazir* 23b; *Targum Yonatan, Ruth* 1.
19. *Zohar, Balak* 104; *Etz Chayyim.*
20. *Zohar, Balak* 104; *Tomer Devorah* (by R. Mosheh ben Ya'akov Cordovero).
21. T. *Sotah* 47a; T. *Sanhedrin* 105b.
22. *Seder Olam Rabbah.*
23. *Me'am Lo'ez.*
24. T. *Sanhedrin* 56a.

25. *Ruth Rabbah* 1; Malbim, *Ruth* 1:4; *Iggeret Shemu'el* (by R. Shemu'el ben Yitzchak Uceda).

26. *Shocher Tov.*

27. Ramban, *Genesis* 16:3; T. *Yevamot* 64a; Targum Yonatan, *Ruth* 1.

28. *Me'am Lo'ez.*

29. *Ruth Rabbah* 1; see also Vilna Ga'on (R. Eliyyahu ben Shelomoh Zalman of Vilna), *Ruth* 1.

30. Malbim, *Ruth* 1:6; *Pardes Rimmonim* (by R. Mosheh ben Ya'akov Cordovero).

31. *Ruth Rabbah* 1; Malbim, *Ruth* 1:6.

32. *Malbim, Ruth* 1:6; *Einei Mosheh* (by R. Mosheh Alshekh); *Iggeret Shemu'el.*

33. *Shocher Tov; Me'am Lo'ez*

34. *Shocher Tov; Me'am Lo'ez; Ruth Rabbah* 1; T. *Sotah* 42b.

35. T. *Sotah* 42b.

36. Targum Yonatan, *Ruth* 1; *Ruth Rabbah* 1.

37. T. *Yevamot* 47b.

38. *Me'am Lo'ez.*

39. T. *Sotah* 33b.

40. *Ruth Rabbah* 1.

41. T. *Avodah Zarah* 11a; *Bereshit Rabbah* 70; *Tanchuma, Mishpatim.*

42. T. *Yevamot* 47b, including Rashi; Rashi, *Ruth* 1:16; *Ruth Rabbah* 1.

43. J.T. *Ketubbot* 1a; Rashi, *Ruth* 1:19; *Ruth Rabbah* 1; T. *Bava Batra* 15b.

44. *Ruth Rabbah* 1; *Iggeret Shemu'el*; Malbim, *Ruth* 1:19; Rashi, *Ruth* 1:19.

45. *Ruth Rabbah* 1; R. Avraham Yitzchak ha-Kohen Kook, *Iggerot ha-Re'ayah* (Jerusalem: Mosad ha-Rav Kook 1985).

46. *Lekach Tov* (by R. Toviyyah ben Eli'ezer); Vilna Ga'on, *Ruth* 1.

Chapter 2

1. M. *Avot* 4:1; Ramban, *Exodus* 18:21; Malbim, *Ruth* 2:1.

2. *Yalkut Shimoni, Ruth* 3:10; *Nachalat Yosef, Ruth* 2:1 (by R. Yosef Lipowitz).

3. Ramban, *Exodus* 18:21; Malbim, *Ruth* 2:1.

4. See *Ecclesiastes* 9:14; see also T. *Nedarim* 32b.

5. Rashi, *Ruth* 2:1.

6. Ibid.; *Yalkut Shimoni, Ruth* 1:19; *Iggeret Shemu'el*; Rashi, *Ruth* 1:19; T. *Bava Batra* 91a; J.T.*Ketubbot* A.

7. T. *Bava Batra* 91a.

8. *Nachalat Yosef, Ruth* 2:1.

9. *Einei Mosheh, Ruth* 2:1.

10. *Einei Mosheh, Ruth* 2:2; *Shoresh Yishai* (by R. Shelomoh Alkabez); Malbim, *Ruth* 2:2.

11. Rashbam (R. Shemu'el ben Me'ir), T. *Bava Batra* 110a; Radak (R. David Kimchi), *Micah* 5:6; see also Rashi, *Proverbs* 6:26.

12. *Einei Mosheh, Ruth* 2:2; Malbim, *Ruth* 2:2.

13. *Ruth Rabbah* 2; *Einei Mosheh, Ruth* 2:2; Malbim, *Ruth* 2:2; *Shoresh Yishai*.

14. *Iggeret Shemu'el*; *Yalkut Shimoni, Ruth* 2:2.

15. *Nachalat Yosef, Ruth* 2:1; R. Shlomo Aviner, *Megillat Rut* (Beth El: Sifriyat Beit El, 1997), *Ruth* 2:2.

16. *Leviticus* 19:9; M. *Pe'ah* 8:1; Rambam, *Hilkhot Matanot Aniyyim* 1:4–8; T. *Ta'anit* 6b.

17. Rambam, *Hilkhot Matanot Aniyyim* 1:2, 1:4–8.

18. Rashi, *Leviticus* 23:22; M. *Pe'ah* 1:2, 8:5.

19. M. *Pe'ah* 8:5; Rambam, *Hilkhot Matanot Aniyyim* 1:4.

20. Rambam, *Hilkhot Matanot Aniyyim* 1:4, 9:13.

21. Rashbam, T. *Pesachim* 99b.

22. M. *Pe'ah* 5; T. *Menachot* 103b; T. *Ta'anit* 6b; *Arba'ah Turim, Yoreh De'ah* (by R. Ya'akov ben Asher) 253; Rambam, *Hilkhot Matanot Aniyyim* 1–8.

23. *Iggerot Mosheh, Yoreh De'ah* (by R. Mosheh Feinstein).

24. Rambam, *Hilkhot Matanot Aniyyim* 9; *Einei Mosheh, Ruth* 2:10; *Shoresh Yishai; Ruth Rabbah* 2.

25. *Shoresh Yishai; Lekach Tov; Chullin* 7a; *Shabbat* 113a.

26. Tosafot, T. *Nazir* 23b; *Iggeret Shemu'el; Nachalat Yosef, Ruth* 2:3; Malbim, *Ruth* 2:3.

27. T. *Shabbat* 113a.

28. *Iggeret Shemu'el;* Malbim, *Ruth* 2:3.

29. *Yalkut Shimoni, Ruth* 2:3; *Ruth Rabbah* 2; Rashi, *Ruth* 2:3.

30. *Lekach Tov; Ruth Rabbah* 2; *Nachalat Yosef, Ruth* 2:3; see also Ya'akov ben Asher, *Numbers* 23:4–5; Ramban, *Numbers* 23:4–5.

31. T. *Chullin* 7a-b; *Nachalat Yosef, Ruth* 2:3.

32. Rambam, *Hilkhot Teshuvah* 5:5; Rambam, *Moreh Nevukhim* (*Guide of the Perplexed*) 3:18.

33. *Nachalat Yosef, Ruth* 2:3.
34. Malbim, *Ruth* 2:4; *Einei Mosheh, Ruth* 2:4.
35. M. *Berakhot* 9:5.
36. *Shabbat* 10b; see also Rambam, end of M. *Berakhot*; *She'elot Shelomoh* (by Shelomoh Zalman Segal) 6:36a.
37. *Job* 2:11–13; *Shulchan Arukh* 193, 207; *Gesher Ha-Chayyim* (by R. Yechi'el Michel Tuchachinsky), chapter 16.
38. Rashi, *Ruth* 2:5; *Iggeret Shemu'el*; T. *Shabbat* 113b; *Ruth Rabbah* 4.
39. Vilna Ga'on, *Ruth* 2.
40. *Yalkut Shimoni, Ruth* 2:8; *Einei Mosheh, Ruth* 2:8.
41. Ramban, *Genesis* 24:51; Don Yitzchak Abravanel, *Leviticus* 23:22.
42. *Iggeret Shemu'el*; *Zohar Chadash*.
43. Yavetz (R. Ya'akov Emden), *Ruth* 2.
44. *Shoresh Yishai*.
45. Ibid.
46. Ramban, *Genesis* 24:51; Malbim, *Ruth* 2:9; *Einei Mosheh, Ruth* 2:8.
47. T. *Menachot* 103b; T. *Ta'anit* 6b; Rambam, *Hilkhot Matanot Aniyyim* 1–4; Arba'ah Turim, *Yoreh De'ah* 253.
48. T. *Yevamot* 69a, 76b; T. *Bava Kamma* 38b; T. *Sanhedrin* 106b; R. Re'uven Margali'ot, *Ha-Mikra ve-ha-Masorah* (Tel Aviv: Yavneh, 1964), pages 20–22.
49. Targum Yonatan, *Ruth* 2; *Shoresh Yishai*.
50. *Lekach Tov*; *Ruth Rabbah* 2; *Zohar Chadash*.

51. *Yalkut Shimoni*, *Ruth* 2:9; Targum Yonatan, *Ruth* 2.
52. Targum Yonatan, *Ruth* 2; *Einei Mosheh*, *Ruth* 2:12.
53. T. *Gittin* 70a; Rambam, *Hilkhot De'ot* 5.
54. Malbim, *Ruth* 2: 17.
55. Rashi, *Exodus* 16:36; T. *Eruvin* 83b.
56. *Einei Mosheh*, *Ruth* 2:19; *Iggeret Shemu'el*.
57. *Ruth Rabbah* 5:9; *Yalkut Shimoni*, *Ruth* 2:12; M. *Pe'ah* 8:9.
58. Malbim, *Ruth* 2:19; *Chovot ha-Levavot* (*Duties of the Heart*, by R. Bachya ben Yosef ibn Pakuda) 2.
59. *Shoresh Yishai*; *Iggeret Shemu'el*; *Einei Mosheh*, *Ruth* 2:20; Malbim, *Ruth* 2:20.
60. Rashi, *Ruth* 3:9; Targum Yonatan, *Ruth* 2.
61. *Iggeret Shemu'el*, *Ruth* 4:3; see also Ibn Ezra, *Leviticus* 25; Ibn Ezra, *Ruth* 4:3; T. *Bava Kamma* 108a; *Einei Mosheh*, *Ruth* 2:20.
62. Ramban, *Genesis* 38:8; Zohar, *Va-Yeshev* 187b; Tosafot, T. *Ketubbot* 7a; *Zohar Chadash*.
63. *Ruth Rabbah* 2; *Iggeret Shemu'el*.
64. Ibn Ezra, *Ruth* 2; Yavetz, *Ruth* 2; *Shoresh Yishai*; *Einei Mosheh*, *Ruth* 2:21.
65. *Iggeret Shemu'el*; *Ruth Rabbah* 2; *Nachalat Yosef*, *Ruth* 2:23.
66. *Shulchan Arukh*, *Even ha-Ezer* 13a.

Chapter 3

1. *Einei Mosheh*, *Ruth* 3:1.
2. *Ruth Rabbah* 3.

3. *Einei Mosheh*, Ruth 3:1.

4. Ibn Ezra, *Ruth* 3; Malbim, *Ruth* 3:1.

5. T. *Bava Batra* 75a.

6. *Ruth Rabbah* 3; see also Rashi, *Ruth* 4:13.

7. *Yalkut Shimoni*, Ruth 1:19; see also Rashi, *Ruth* 1:19.

8. Ibn Ezra, *Ruth* 3; Malbim, *Ruth* 3:3.

9. *Genesis* 1:9; *Leviticus* 8:6, 11:29–38, 14:7–9, 15:5–13; *Eruvin* 14a–b; *Pesachim* 16a; Dr. Me'ir Ben-Dov, *Ha-Kotel* (Jerusalem: Israel Ministry of Defense, 1984), 196.

10. Rashi, *Ruth* 2:20; Zohar, *Vayeshev 134*; see also *Ezekiel* 16:9–10; R. Feivel Meltzer, *Da'at Mikra* (Jerusalem: Mosad ha-Rav Kook, 1973).

11. Malbim, *Ruth* 3:3; Ramban, *Genesis* 38:8.

12. T. *Shabbat* 113b; J.T. *Pe'ah* 8; *Ruth Rabbah* 5:12.

13. Ralbag (R. Levi ben Gershom) *Ruth* 4; *Iggeret Shemu'el*.

14. T. *Nazir* 23b; R. Avraham Yitzchak ha-Kohen Kook, *Mishpat Kohen* (Jerusalem: Mosad ha-Rav Kook, 1971), page 316; R. Aviner, *Megillat Rut*, Ruth 3:3–4.

15. Zohar, *Vayeshev* 109; Malbim, *Ruth* 3:3–4.

16. *Shulchan Arukh, Orach Chayyim* 141:8; *Yalkut Shimoni*, Ruth 3:5; *Minchat Shai* (by R. Shelomoh Yedidyah).

17. *Shoresh Yishai*.

18. *Etz Chayyim*; Zohar, *Bereshit* 138.

19. T. *Sanhedrin* 19b.

20. *Ruth Rabbah* 3; *Lekach Tov*.

21. *Einei Mosheh, Ruth* 3:10.
22. Rashi, *Ruth* 3:12.
23. Malbim, *Ruth* 3:13; *Shoresh Yishai.*
24. *Shoresh Yishai.*
25. Ibid.; *Iggeret Shemu'el.*
26. T. *Sanhedrin* 93a, including Rashi; *Ezekiel* 46; Malbim, *Ruth* 3:15; Ibn Ezra, *Ruth* 3; Targum Yonatan, *Ruth* 3; *Midrash ha-Gadol* (by R. David ben Amram of Aden).
27. T. *Sanhedrin* 93a-b; Rashi, *Ruth* 3:15; *1 Samuel* 16–18; *Isaiah* 11:1; *Shoresh Yishai.*
28. Rashi, *Bereshit* 18:13; T. *Bava Metzi'a* 87a; R. Aviner, *Megillat Rut, Ruth* 3:17.
29. *Iggeret Shemu'el.*
30. T. *Sukkah* 46b.
31. Ibn Ezra, *Ruth* 3; Targum Yonatan, *Ruth* 3.

Chapter 4

1. T. *Sotah* 37a.
2. *Iggeret Shelomoh* (by R. Shelomoh Zalman Segal).
3. *Einei Mosheh, Ruth* 4:1.
4. Ramban, *Genesis* 38:8, *Deuteronomy* 25:6.
5. *Shoresh Yishai; Ruth Rabbah* 7:6.
6. T. *Ketubbot* 7b; *Ruth Rabbah* 7:7; *Yalkut Shimoni, Ruth* 4:2; *Shoresh Yishai;* see also *Genesis* 18:32.
7. Malbim, *Ruth* 4:4; *Einei Mosheh, Ruth* 4:4.
8. Targum Yonatan, *Ruth* 4.
9. *Einei Mosheh, Ruth* 4:6; Malbim, *Ruth* 4:6; Ralbag; *Shoresh Yishai; Ruth Rabbah* 4:6.

10. T. *Yevamot* 6b; *Shulchan Arukh*, 169–170.
11. Malbim, *Ruth* 4:9–10.
12. *Ruth Zuta* 4:9; *Shocher Tov.*
13. See *Einei Mosheh, Ruth* 4:11–12.
14. Malbim, *Ruth* 4:11.
15. Ibid.; *Iggeret Shemu'el.*
16. T. *Bava Metzi'a* 58b; *Einei Mosheh, Ruth* 4:11.
17. *Yalkut Shimoni, Ruth* 4:13.
18. *Ruth Zuta* 4:13; *Yalkut Shimoni, Ruth* 4:13; *Sefer Chasidim* (by R. Yehudah ben Shemu'el he-Cha-sid).
19. *Zohar Chadash.*
20. Ibid.
21. *Einei Moshe, Ruth* 4:16.
22. Malbim, *Ruth* 4:16.
23. T. *Sanhedrin* 19b; Maharsha (R. Shemu'el Eli'ezer Edels), T. *Sanhedrin* 19b; *Zohar Chadash, Ki Tetze* 59a.
24. M. *Avot* 6.
25. R. Abraham Joshua Heschel, *God in Search of Man* (New York: Farrar Straus & Giroux, 1955), chapters 20 and 42; R. Abraham Joshua Heschel, *Man Is Not Alone* (New York: Farrar Straus & Giroux, 1951), chapters 14, 16, and 24.
26. Rambam, *Moreh Nevukhim*, 52–56.

Suggested Reading

Aviner, Shlomo. *Megillat Rut.* Beth El: Sifriyat Beit El, 1997.

Bachrach, Yehoshua. *Ruth: Mother of Royalty.* New York: Feldheim Publishers, 1973.

Broch, Yitzhak I. *Ruth: The Book of Ruth in Hebrew and English with a Midrashic Commentary.* New York: Feldheim Publishers, 1983.

Cohen, A., ed. *The Five Megilloth.* Surrey, UK: Soncino Press, 1946.

Davis, Avrohom, and Yaakov Y. H. Pupko, trans. *The Metsudah Five Megillos.* Brooklyn: Metsudah Publications, 2001.

Kolatch, Alfred J. *The Second Jewish Book of Why.* New York: Jonathan David Publishers, Inc., 2000.

Levin, Malka. *The Interview.* Jerusalem: Jewish Treasures, 1988.

Malbim, Meir Leibush. *Malbim on Ruth.* Translated by Shmuel Kurtz. New York: Feldheim Publishers, 1999.

Masliansky, Zevi Hirsch. *Sermons.* New York: Hebrew Publishing Co., 1926.

Meltzer, Feivel. *Da'at Mikra.* Jerusalem: Mosad ha-Rav Kook, 1973.

Mindel, Nissan. *Complete Story of Shovuoth.* Seventh ed. Brooklyn: Merkos L'Inyonei Chinuch, 1963.

Scherman, Nosson, ed. *The Book of Ruth.* Second ed. Brooklyn: Mesorah Publications, 1976.

Simhoni, S. *Legends of Ruth: Retold for Jewish Youth.* Translated by I. M. Lask. New York: Shulsinger Brothers, 1962.

Touger, Malka, ed. *Me'am Lo'ez for Youth: Ruth.* New York: Moznaim, 1988.

Tzukernik, Shimonah, ed. *A Teacher's Treasure: The Lectures of Rebbetzin Heller: Megillas Rus.* Brooklyn: Bais Rivkah Seminary Division of Higher Learning, 2003.

Yerushalmi, Shmuel. *The Torah Anthology: Me'am Lo'ez: The Book of Ruth.* Translated by E. van Handel. Edited by Zvi Faier. New York: Moznaim, 1989.

Temple Israel

Minneapolis, Minnesota

TN HONOR OF
THE 85TH BIRTHDAY OF
NORMAN BLOOM
FROM
MR. & MRS. EDWIN HARRIS